Praise for
Jennifer Goldman-Wetzler
and Optimal Outcomes

"Jennifer captivated our audience of Googlers . . . Her high-energy presentation was bursting with extremely clear and practical advice on how to master even the most difficult conflicts. I recommend her to anyone planning an event anywhere."

—Rachael O'Meara, Google

"A brilliantly written guide for the twenty-first-century leader. Jennifer Goldman-Wetzler will change how you think about conflict and complexity and, more importantly, how you lead through both."

—Sharon Fay, cohead of equities, AllianceBernstein

"*Optimal Outcomes* provides a simple but powerful method for dealing with breakdowns that seem unresolvable."

—Erica Ariel Fox, president of Mobius Executive Leadership
and author of the *New York Times* bestseller *Winning from Within*

"An important, unique approach to dealing with conflict, even when one side may not be amenable. Highly recommended for anyone interested in applying a user-friendly methodology in their personal and professional interactions."

—Joshua Sinai, PhD, counterterrorism expert, book reviews editor for
Perspectives on Terrorism, and columnist for the *Washington Times*

"Optimal Outcomes is a method whose time has come. It is useful wherever conflict has lasted too long, including in the Middle East. The practices will help everyone from diplomats to grassroots organizers break cycles of conflict and taste freedom."

—David Broza, legendary Israeli singer-songwriter and creator of the humanitarian documentary *East Jerusalem/West Jerusalem*

"Jennifer and her course have consistently received the highest ratings across the board. She is highly engaging and her work is transformative. She is a gem at Columbia, not to be missed."

—Dr. Peter T. Coleman, professor of psychology and education and executive director of the Morton Deutsch International Center for Cooperation and Conflict Resolution at Columbia University

"After years of teaching her groundbreaking ideas to Columbia students, Jennifer Goldman-Wetzler makes them available to the rest of us for the first time. Enjoy!"

—Amy Elizabeth Fox, CEO of Mobius Executive Leadership

"Our entire company has benefitted tremendously from Jennifer Goldman-Wetzler's expertise. She has provided us with the frank insight and leadership know-how to significantly develop our organizational culture. The successful selling of our company to the most prestigious brand in our industry is partially attributable to Jennifer's advisory."

—Allan Weiser, CEO of DatesWeiser/Knoll Specialty

"Framed with . . . a kind but no-nonsense tone, this succinct and focused guide is a boon to anyone looking to turn arguments into negotiations and negotiations into agreement."

—*Publishers Weekly*

Optimal
Outcomes

Free Yourself from Conflict
at Work, at Home, and in Life

Optimal
Outcomes

Jennifer Goldman-Wetzler, PhD

HARPER
BUSINESS

An Imprint of HarperCollins*Publishers*

HarperCollins books may be purchased for educational, business, or sales promotional use. For information, please email the Special Markets Department at SPsales@harpercollins.com.

Conflict map reprinted with permission from Robert Louis-Charles.

FIRST EDITION

Illustration by Jutta Kuss/Getty Images

Library of Congress Cataloging-in-Publication Data has been applied for.

ISBN 978-0-06-289365-9

20 21 22 23 24   LSC   10 9 8 7 6 5 4 3 2 1

For my family

Contents

✳

PART I

Understanding the Conflict Loop

Introduction

﹡

I had been teaching executive leaders and graduate students to free themselves from recurring conflict for years before I decided to take on one of the persistent challenges in my adult life.

I love my mother dearly. She is my rock, my biggest supporter, and often the first person I go to for counsel. Still, a few years ago, a long-simmering conflict between us exploded. I'm embarrassed now to admit it, but I gave her the classic "shape up or ship out" ultimatum, delivered via the central medium of our conflict: the cell phone. From my home office, I screamed at her, flung down the phone, and burst into tears. Twenty miles away in her apartment in the Bronx, my mom stewed in her own fury.

My threat was made in the heat of anger, and I later retracted it, after a week spent feeling angry, guilty, and unable to focus on anything else.

What got me so upset? My mom called me on the phone. If that sounds harmless, allow me to explain.

As with most working parents, each day is a delicate Rube Goldberg machine of moving parts; if I shift my attention away, missing one of the steps of the sequence, the ball drops and the game is over. At least it seems that way.

When my mother called me, often in the middle of the day's hectic march—which is to say, between 6:00 a.m. and 9:00 p.m.—I often responded with a huffy "I'm sorry, Mom, I don't have much time to talk right now."

My mother did not like that answer. "But you never call me! How can you not have time for your mother?" she'd ask. Often, complaining about my not calling was the singular purpose of her call.

That happened again and again. At some point, I stopped answering most of her calls. That made her even more critical and carping about a wider range of things, which made me even more combative.

As often happens, one fight led to another and the conflict became harder and harder for my mother and me to escape. And each time a flare-up occurred, our relationship was diminished, bit by bit. This was almost inevitable.

The day I committed to breaking free from our conflict loop, I didn't make the commitment in private. I did it standing before a seminar of twenty graduate students and four teaching assistants in my class on Optimal Outcomes at Columbia University. I hoped using this real, raw episode in my life would help my students see that the practices I'd be presenting over the course of the three-day workshop could successfully be applied to any conflict, no matter how close or seemingly cataclysmic. I also wanted them to understand that good things come from making yourself vulnerable.

But I was still nervous. I was opening myself up to a seminar full of graduate students, who at that point were still strangers to me.

Would they think it was odd to dedicate class time to my mother and me? Would my being so personal alienate them?

I found out quickly that I had nothing to fear. As I described our conflict in more detail—which I'll do for you, too, a bit later—I saw heads nodding and eyes sparkling with engagement.

Of course they got it. Aside from the fact that they had parental figures in their own lives, they also had conflicts so potent, so frustrating, that they had gone to tough places, too.

Me, you, and everyone: we all deal with conflict all the time. It doesn't matter how much we love our family, respect our colleagues, or like our neighbors. Conflict happens.

You do your best to manage it well, of course. Sometimes your efforts pay off. Other times, no matter what you do, the same problem keeps coming back again and again *and again* despite your best attempts to resolve it.

Like me, you feel stuck. You've tried everything.

And you're at a complete loss for what to do next.

That's where I was the day I let my students into my story. Being stuck in conflict was taking time and energy that I wanted to spend in an affirming way with the people I cared about, including my mother. Instead, everywhere I went I was thinking about the situation: while brushing my teeth, commuting, putting my kids to sleep, listening to people who had come to me for counsel. I was even dreaming about it.

Let's face it: being stuck in conflict can make it difficult to be present with what you're doing and contribute the way you'd like to the people and world around you.

If any of this sounds familiar, the first thing I want you to understand is that you're not alone. Getting stuck in conflict is prevalent—even among the most seasoned leaders in business, academia, and government, some of whom I've consulted with and whose stories I share throughout this book.

I have changed identifying details such as names and industries to protect my clients' and students' privacy. However, each of these stories reflects my experience working with leaders on some of the toughest problems they've faced in their professional and personal lives.

How I Got Here

In my work as an organizational psychologist at the company I founded, Alignment Strategies Group, I've used the Optimal Outcomes Method over the past thirteen years to help turn around challenging situations facing executives at some of the world's leading organizations, universities, and public institutions. As a professor, I've spent more than a decade teaching the Optimal Outcomes Method to midcareer professionals and students who come to Columbia University's Morton Deutsch International Center for Cooperation and Conflict Resolution from an array of Columbia's graduate schools: business, international affairs, psychology, education, religion, and law. At the end of the three-day workshop, people who entered the room grappling with daunting conflicts leave revitalized with fresh perspective and a new sense of freedom.

I have written this book with the hopes that it will bring that sense of freedom to you as well.

The Optimal Outcomes Method reaches beyond what you may have encountered if you've read books on conflict resolution in the past. In my early career, I served as a facilitator at Harvard Law School's Program on Negotiation (PON), the world's most respected resource on dispute resolution and negotiation. That put me into the classrooms and conference rooms of two men who today remain giants in the field: the late Roger Fisher (who coauthored the seminal *Getting to Yes: Negotiating Agreement Without Giving In* in 1981) and Bruce Patton (a coauthor of *Getting to Yes* and also of the 1999 game changer *Difficult Conversations: How to Discuss What Matters Most*, whose firm I joined around the time the latter book was published). I had worked hard to get there, and it was an exciting, dynamic time, as Fisher and those he influenced moved the field away from competitive, winner-take-all-style negotiation to the collaborative, we-all-can-win approach that thankfully persists today.

It was a formative experience for me, yet as the years passed, I found myself asking questions that weren't adequately addressed by the methods I was teaching. My academic background was in social psychology, but surrounded by lawyers, I began to notice that my colleagues saw conflict and its resolution as infinitely possible but tangible and finite. Every case had an end. Yet when I looked around at my own life and at the world's most destructive struggles, I saw conflicts that seemed intractable, often resurfacing most violently just when resolution seemed near. For example, after several hopeful years of negotiations facilitated by a team of international diplomats who had been trained in "win-win" methods, the Oslo peace process between Israelis and Palestinians broke down and renewed cycles of violence took its place.

I wondered whether there was any hope for people who couldn't seem to negotiate their way to resolution through the "win-win" methods I had been advancing.

I was also intrigued by how emotions such as anger and sadness contribute to conflict. I had grown up in a family of screamers and door slammers, of which my grandfather was the most extreme example. He had fled Vienna in 1938 in anticipation of the Nazi invasion, and he had eventually landed in New York, where he had rebuilt his life. Today I can just barely comprehend the pain he endured, the grief and guilt of leaving people he loved behind forever. He never saw his father again. One of his brothers remained in Europe and was murdered by the Nazis for refusing to turn in other Jews. Two of his other brothers ended up in Australia, safe but far-flung for the rest of their lives. My grandfather never spoke about his pain, but I believe I experienced the visceral effects of his repressing it: occasional bouts of anger and rage that many times left me and my little brother cowering in a corner of his apartment in the Bronx.

On the other side of my family, my maternal grandmother, Florence, was the quintessential conflict whisperer. All she had to do was say, "Shh, shh," which was her gentle way of quieting us down, and everyone would become calm. I suspect that learning how to deal with my grandfather's anger, and being inspired by my grandmother's calming influence, helped me to become a calming presence for my family, too, and eventually for my clients, students, and friends. I hope not only to be that presence for you in these pages but also to teach you how to become that kind of force in your own life.

My desire to understand seemingly intractable conflict led me to the PhD program in social-organizational psychology at Columbia University in September 2002, where I found others exploring similar questions. One year after the 9/11 terrorist attacks, I was granted a graduate research fellowship by the US Department of Homeland Security and spent the next five years studying the effects of humiliation on aggression in the context of conflicts such as global terrorism.

It was a journey deep into the emotional causes of serious long-term conflict. I spent time on the ground in the Middle East with Palestinian, Jordanian, and Israeli teachers and students facilitating dialogue and cross-border relationships. And I discovered research that spoke to the experiences I'd had with my grandfather regarding how painful emotions such as anger and humiliation contribute to aggressive behavior, which in turn often causes further aggression, perpetuating cycles of devastating conflict.

Today, as an organizational psychologist, I help leaders deal productively with their anger so it doesn't come out in aggressive bursts as my grandfather's did. I also help people learn to deal with *others'* anger-fueled attacks productively, so that everyone grows from the experience. In these pages, you'll meet some of my clients, and I hope and trust you'll find their stories illuminating and helpful.

Conflict *Can* Be Good for You

Getting stuck in conflict is common partly because conflict itself is inevitable.

Generally speaking, conflict is a natural, normal, healthy part of everyday life. For example, according to the renowned marriage researcher John Gottman, the presence of *some* amount of conflict in a marriage (as opposed to none or too much) is a typical marker of a happy, healthy relationship.

Conflict can also be productive and lead to innovative solutions. For instance, diverse teams, in which team members engage in conflict as a result of naturally arising differing perspectives, have been found to be more creative, innovative, and productive than teams in which everyone looks, sounds, and thinks alike.

Interesting plotlines in books, plays, and movies—and to some degree life itself—depend on the protagonist facing an inner or outer conflict and learning how to overcome it. For example, think of the main characters in the world's best-known pieces of literature, from Gilgamesh to Moses, from Mohammed to the Buddha, all of whom face and overcome gargantuan conflicts—both inside themselves and with others. The renowned mythologist Joseph Campbell has noted the archetypical nature of these stories. He offers us the language of the "hero's journey," where the main character must wrestle with an inner conflict or a conflict with someone or something else that is difficult to control. Campbell says that what makes life interesting and worth living is for each of us to meet and overcome the inner and outer conflicts that inevitably appear along our paths in life.

In short, without conflict, the world would be a much less productive, less interesting, perhaps even less worthwhile place.

Some conflict—a healthy amount of it—is and should remain part of a well-functioning life, team, organization, or society.

However, conflict that returns no matter how many times you try to resolve it tends not to contribute to your health and growth. Instead, it makes it hard to enjoy life or achieve your goals.

Conflict Begets Conflict

In the 1970s, Dr. Morton Deutsch, widely considered the father of conflict resolution, made a simple but profound discovery about the nature of conflict: it's self-perpetuating. Specifically, through a series of experiments, he found that once a conflict begins, by its very nature, it is likely to lead to more conflict.

For example, when we experience conflict with someone else, we tend to think, feel, and act in ways that cause more conflict, which leads to thoughts, feelings, and actions that cause more conflict, and so on. Throughout this book, we'll explore several reasons *why* conflict leads to more conflict. For now, let's simply note that conflict recurrence is the nature of the beast. I call it the *conflict loop*.

What I've discovered is that when you're stuck in a conflict loop, you develop conflict habits, including blaming or avoiding others, blaming yourself, and relentlessly seeking "win-win" solutions even when other people refuse to cooperate. And your conflict habits interact with other people's conflict habits to form a pattern of interaction that keeps you stuck in the conflict loop.

After five years in graduate school studying the factors that contribute to intractable conflict, I understood something about how we get ourselves stuck in a conflict loop. What I still didn't know then was: *How can we get ourselves out?*

But now, over more than a decade, I have helped leaders free themselves from recurring conflicts. This book describes a method, grounded in research and practice, that will help you do the same.

The Optimal Outcomes Method

The Optimal Outcomes Method is a set of eight practices you can use to free yourself from the habits and patterns that reinforce the conflict loop.

In Practice 1, I help you notice and stop engaging in the often unconscious habits that make conflict worse, such as avoiding it until it explodes, acting in the heat of the moment in ways you'll later regret, blaming yourself unnecessarily, or relentlessly seeking to collaborate even when others are not willing to do so.

In Practices 2, 3, and 4, I show you how to step back from a conflict, no matter how heated it may be, and observe it so you can figure out what's really causing it. Doing this gives you new insight into the situation, which helps you break the conflict pattern by taking constructive action that is different from what you've done before.

In Practices 5, 6, 7, and 8, I help you imagine, design, test, and choose a new path to an Optimal Outcome—which sometimes substantially differs from what you once thought would be an ideal outcome. Though you might begin the process with firm ideas of how your conflict *should* be resolved, an Optimal Outcome will likely bring you greater personal satisfaction and more lasting harmony than your original goal ever could have.

In order for the practices to free you from the habits that you may (intentionally or not) have spent years honing, you'll need to practice them, sometimes over and over again, to build your proficiency.

Before we explore the eight practices in depth, we need to acknowledge two fundamentals of the Optimal Outcomes Method that are woven throughout each practice: developing the capacity to *observe* and taking *pattern-breaking action*.

Pause to Observe

Today, mindfulness—learning to stay engaged with the present moment—has been widely acknowledged as a valuable tool to break free from past experiences and future expectations, so that we can better experience the here and now. *Pausing* is a mindfulness practice that enhances your awareness of wherever you are. It helps you notice the nuances in a situation that are easy to miss when you approach life from a less attentive state. Pausing helps you see things from a different perspective. It also allows you to acknowledge what is happening *without needing to change it*, which is, paradoxically, essential to freeing yourself from conflict.

Pausing is about taking a moment to notice what *is*. I'll show you how to do this throughout the book. Whether you've spent years sitting quietly on a meditation cushion or you've never taken a moment's pause before, the practices in this book are deep enough to provide you with new insight and simple enough to be done by anyone.

Take Pattern-Breaking Action

The purpose of pausing is ultimately to help you not only identify but also to break the pattern and free yourself from the conflict loop. As I'll explain in a moment, pausing often breaks the conflict pattern all by itself, while at other times pausing happens first and pattern-breaking action follows.

In part I of the book, pausing will help you recognize how your own conflict habits interact with others' to form a conflict pattern. Sometimes, pausing to observe a conflict situation will be pattern breaking in and of itself. If you've been taking action to try to make the conflict go away, just observing it will break the pattern.

The practices in part II of the book will help you break free from the conflict pattern by *first* pausing to acknowledge the factors that have contributed to it so you can *then* take pattern-breaking action. Pattern-breaking action happens when you create a new response to a familiar scenario. This will help you start moving in a different direction.

In part III, you'll pause to imagine your Ideal Future (a "prototype" of an Optimal Outcome); then you'll design a Pattern-Breaking Path to move you toward your Ideal Future; and finally, you'll turn your prototyped Ideal Future into an Optimal Outcome so you can exit the conflict loop for good.

What Is an Optimal Outcome?

In recurring conflicts, we tend not to be very good at imagining what we want. Instead, we're focused on what went wrong in the past and who is to blame. If we do think about the future, we tend not to look honestly at the reality we're facing. (It's much easier to fantasize about idealized scenarios that could never happen in real life than to face up to the often cold, hard reality of other people's experiences, desires, and needs.) To account for this, as figure 1 illustrates, the degree to which you are able to create an Optimal Outcome is determined *both* by your ability to imagine an Ideal Future *and* to acknowledge the reality of the situation and people you're dealing with. We will explore how to distinguish fantasy from reality in Practices 1 and 8.

Breaking free from a conflict loop can be challenging. The habits and patterns that reinforce it have a strong inward pull. In order to break free, you'll need a force from outside the loop to pull you out. The Optimal Outcome is that force, and in Practice 8, I'll show you how to create it to pull you away from the conflict loop and toward freedom.

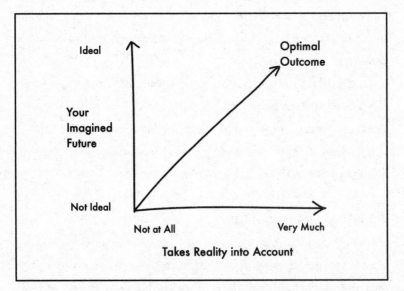

FIGURE 1: An Optimal Outcome maximizes your imagined future and reality.

What Is Conflict Freedom, Anyway?

With all this talk about freeing yourself from conflict, I need to be clear about something: The goal of this book is *not* to help you rid yourself of all conflict. Instead, when your repeated attempts to resolve conflict fail, the practices in this book will help you notice and free yourself from the habitual ways of thinking, feeling, and acting that have held you captive in the past. This will help you free yourself from the conflict loop in any given situation.

The beauty of having conflict freedom as your goal is that *you already have the ability to become free within yourself.* You don't need to wait for anyone else to change or to agree with you. *You can free yourself even without anyone else's cooperation.*

Similarly, though help from skilled people can be useful if you have access to it, in most cases, you don't need a coach, talent management professional, or mediator in order to become free. You can achieve an Optimal Outcome on your own. The practices in this book will show you how.

When you break free from a conflict loop that's had a hold on you, there's a moment when you'll suddenly feel free—physically lighter, exhaling a huge sigh of relief, and free from the sense of powerlessness that kept you stuck before.

When I experienced that magical moment myself in the situation with my mom, I felt the release of physical tension in my body—the sudden lightness in my step, the unclenching of my jaw. I've witnessed these changes with my students and clients as well. Their shoulders broaden and relax; their mouths turn from frowning to smiling; their scrunched-up brows become smooth. There's a physical and emotional freedom that accompanies conflict freedom.

I know this is possible for you, too.

A Note About Language

This book is about how to become free from conflict, and I've found that language can either help or hinder that process. Research on priming suggests that how we describe people and situations influences the way we think about and experience them. The words we choose matter.

For example, even using the word *conflict* to describe a situation can influence how you think about it and therefore can impact your outcome. When you hear the word *conflict*, your brain makes connections with similar words such as *fight* and *disagreement* and with concepts such as the idea that conflict must be difficult. As a result of the priming effect, you are more likely to assume that a conflict is inescapable than to look for new ways to approach it.

Similarly, using a conflict-oriented word such as *counterpart*, *party*, or *opponent* to define your relationship with someone doesn't represent the complex nature of most relationships and doesn't leave much room for your relationship with that person to change over time.

I want to leave the door open to the possibility of change, so whenever possible, I try to use more neutral or informal descriptors, such as *brother*, *friend*, *leader*, *colleague*, *them*, *theirs*, or *others*. I have also done my best to use words such as *situation* and *experience* to describe what you're facing. However, sometimes I use the word *conflict* in order to be as clear as possible about what I am talking about. I encourage you to experiment with the words you use and notice how they impact the way you view what is possible.

Given the insidious nature of the priming effect, it may not be realistic to avoid it altogether, but it is worthwhile to try to use language that will support, rather than hinder, what you are trying to achieve. Even simply acknowledging the power of the priming effect has the potential to be helpful.

Identify a Situation to Use Throughout the Book

In my course at Columbia, I ask my students to choose a conflict situation they care about, ideally from their own life, to which they can apply the Optimal Outcomes Method throughout the course. Some students have no problem thinking of one.

But in every class, there are one or two students who have trouble identifying a situation. When I first started teaching the course, one of those students was Jordana, a twenty-eight-year-old manager at a software company from a large family in Maryland.

When Jordana's mind came up blank, I asked about where she worked and lived. Still nothing came to her. Then I asked about her family. After a hesitant pause, she started speaking slowly.

Jordana said, "Well, my parents have been divorced since I was two years old. My father had an affair over twenty years ago, and my mother has never forgiven him. He's been remarried for most of my life, but my mom has been single since they got divorced. They can't stand each other, and whenever they have to talk or see each other, all hell breaks loose. Now my middle sister's wedding is coming up in a few months, and I have no idea how we're going to handle my parents being in the same room for the wedding. And my oldest sister is pregnant. Who will get to be the first to visit the baby in the hospital? Plus I'll be finishing school soon, and I want both of my parents to come to my graduation."

Jordana was like the proverbial fish who can't see the water she's swimming in—because the water is everywhere. She had been living with her parents' conflict since she was two years old. It had surrounded her so completely that she didn't even think of it as conflict; she just thought of it as her life.

Now that she was an adult, she saw how her parents' conflict could make many years of future family gatherings challenging for herself and her two sisters. Once she identified her parents' conflict, she had the power to work with it.

From experience, I know that the best way to understand the Optimal Outcomes practices is to apply them to a situation you care about. That's why, in every chapter, I'll ask you a series of questions to help you apply the practices to *your* situation.

Just as Jordana did, take a moment now to consider a variety of situations in your life. Think about recurring conflict situations you care about at work, in your family, your community, or in the national or international arenas.

In order to get the most out of this book, choose a situation to which the following three statements apply:

1. *I am directly impacted by the situation.* I am not simply an observer in someone else's dispute.

2. *I or someone else has tried to resolve the conflict in the past and failed.*

3. *I can do something to help.* The situation is still happening; it is not a closed case.

If you're still grappling with various different situations, choose the one that is most pressing for you.

Now take a moment to write down your answers to the following questions:

Who is involved in the situation?

What is the conflict about? In other words, what are the people con-cerned about?

Finally, see if you can pinpoint exactly *why* you want to achieve an Optimal Outcome. Your answer will motivate you to do the practices in this book, even when the going gets tough. And it may get tough. At some point, the practices will require you to look honestly at yourself and consider ways you can change to achieve the results you're looking for. This can be difficult even for the most courageous and flexible among us. But research shows that if you know why you are making a change, it can be easier to commit and stick to it. So take a moment to write down your answer to the following question:

Why do I want freedom from this conflict?

Once you know why, the rest of this book will help you focus on *how*: it will help you understand exactly how you got stuck *and* show you how to break free from the conflict loop, even without anyone else's agreement or cooperation. You'll take a hard look at where things stand today, and you'll learn how to free yourself, both now and in the future.

Summary

* Conflict is inevitable. A healthy amount of conflict is part of a well-functioning life, team, organization, or society. However, recurring conflict makes it hard to be present or contribute the way you'd like to the people and world around you.

* By its very nature, conflict begets conflict in a self-reinforcing loop. Once a conflict begins, it is likely to lead to more conflict.

* Not all conflicts can be resolved neatly. In those instances when resolution seems impossible, freeing yourself from the conflict loop first requires simply noticing the conflict pattern. Part I of the book will show you how to do this.

* The practices in part II will help you pause to observe the existing conflict pattern in more depth and then take *pattern-breaking action*. Pattern-breaking action is any constructive action that is *different from* what you've been doing.

* To free yourself from the conflict loop, the practices in part III will help you imagine, design, test, and choose a path to achieve an Optimal Outcome. An Optimal Outcome is an ideal scenario that also takes into account hard truths about the reality of the situation you're facing. It is the force that pulls you away from the conflict loop toward freedom.

Get Started

Choose a recurring conflict that impacts your life so you can apply the practices to it throughout the book. Take a moment now to consider:

* Who is involved in the situation?

* What is the conflict about? In other words, what are the people concerned about?

* Why do you want freedom from this conflict?

✳

Notice Your Conflict Habits and Patterns

In every crisis there is a message. Crises are nature's way of forcing change—breaking down old structures, shaking loose negative habits so that something new and better can take their place.

—SUSAN L. TAYLOR

I n the situation with my mom, each of our conflict habits formed a pattern of interaction that kept us stuck on the conflict loop as if it were a merciless merry-go-round.

Later in this chapter, I'll tell you more about our conflict habits and the pattern we got stuck in, and I'll introduce you to some of my clients' and students' conflict habits and patterns, too. For now, let's look at how conflict habits form in the first place.

How We Develop Conflict Habits

Our conflict habits arise based on how we have been conditioned or taught to approach the world. What we learn from parents and other family members, teachers, sports coaches, religious clergy, and other influential people in our lives has a strong influence on our conflict habits. It is possible to develop our habits explicitly if a prominent figure in our lives tells us how to behave in conflict, but more likely, no one ever talks about these habits with us. They just "model" the way they expect us to behave. We see how they do it, and we take our cues from them.

If you grew up in a house where people yelled, cried, and slammed doors when they were angry (as I did), you might do the same in your own house as an adult (as I admittedly sometimes do). Or if, like my client Stephan, you grew up in a family where the unspoken rule was that conflict is to be avoided at all costs, you may notice that you would rather walk away from a potential conflict than meet it head-on.

We tend to use one habit consistently across multiple contexts. I call this your *primary conflict habit*.

However, your conflict habits *can* depend on the context you're in. You might have one habit at home, another at work, and a third when you're in the community.

The extent to which conflict habits hold across contexts is influenced by the messages you received growing up. For example, I learned from a young age that it was okay to yell and slam doors at home but I should never do so in public. My brother and I routinely fought at home within earshot of our immediate family, but if we even thought about acting like that in the supermarket, our parents put a quick end to it. Today, I am still much more likely to raise my voice at home than in a public setting.

Conflict Habits

Based on research, as well as years of teaching and consulting to organizational leaders, I've identified four conflict habits that, despite our best intentions, keep us stuck in patterns that perpetuate the conflict loop.

As you read through the following descriptions, there may be a moment when you realize that your own habits are part of the problem you're facing. You may feel a defensiveness rising, a "that's not me" voice in your head.

I want you to know that being part of the problem doesn't make you a terrible person. It only makes you human.

If you want to free yourself from conflict, the first practice is to notice how your conflict habits might be contributing to it.

As Doug Stone, Bruce Patton, and Sheila Heen, the authors of the bestselling book *Difficult Conversations: How to Discuss What Matters Most*, put it, whether you are responsible for 5 percent, 50 percent, or 95 percent of the situation you're in isn't the point. The point is that multiple people's contributions have created the situation; you *and* others have jointly contributed to making the situation what it is.

Your primary conflict habit may represent your own contribution to some of the challenging situations you find yourself in.

The good news is that once you understand how your own habit may be getting in your way, you can then choose to stop and do something different. In fact, recent research on individual and organizational learning conducted by researchers at Harvard Business School suggests that performance improves when people reflect on their own behavior. If you acknowledge the way in which you are contributing to a tricky dynamic, you are one step closer to changing the situation for the better.

In part II of this book, I'll show you how to replace your old habits with something new and different. For now, simply recognizing your habit is a critical first practice toward freeing yourself from the conflict loop.

As you read through the descriptions below, keep an open mind and consider which habit is most familiar to you. Each one will probably sound familiar some of the time, but one will stand out as your primary habit: it's what you do when you're not even thinking about it.

Blame Others

Some of us learn from a young age that to get what we want, we need to directly and aggressively pursue it. My client Javier, the founder and CEO of a flashy, award-winning design firm, was one of those people. He was hyperconfident, born into the kind of family that has academic buildings named after them, whose parents celebrated boldness and strength above all other qualities. He was also incredibly talented, which put his self-assurance off the charts.

At his best, his competitive nature was a huge asset. He was a fearless advocate for the company and only too happy to plow through business challenges that might have led other entrepreneurs to weep. For example, his team was in awe of his ability to single-handedly identify, in a matter of minutes, dozens of activities they could pursue to fend off a competitor creeping up on their space. However, there were times he leaned on his competitive spirit too heavily, to the point where it got warped into blaming and attacking others.

Though Javier was an extreme case, many wonderfully competitive spirits, from all kinds of backgrounds, develop the *Blame Others* habit. If that's you, perhaps you've experienced the results of your behavior: other people with strong personalities are liable to

react by counterattacking you, while people who are conflict avoid-
ant shut down completely.

If others counterattack, your competitive spirit leads you to attack back, which only escalates the conflict. Or if they shut down,
you're often stuck, unable to move forward or get what you want
without their agreement or help. Even if you can move ahead on
your own, doing so can lead to more conflict when they learn that
you've done so without them.

In short, the Blame Others habit typically produces a loss rather
than the win you intended. Sometimes you lose face, while other
times you lose money, relationships, time, energy, and focus.

In Javier's case, the Blame Others habit showed its true de-
structiveness in his relationship with Tara, an old friend and his
current head of sales. Tara was a mild Brit who believed in the
power of polite civility and also an über-intelligent entrepreneur
who had the grit needed to exponentially expand the firm's market
share. When he had hired her, Javier had thought she had exactly
the background he needed to help scale up.

However, one day Javier stormed into Tara's office to address
how slowly the hiring process for the sales department was going.
When he loudly blamed her for putting the brakes on poaching talent from another company and then issued new marching orders,
Tara simply shut down. That type of interaction happened repeat-
edly, and whenever it did, the louder he got, the less she heard—and
afterward, she'd stay away from him for as long as she could.

Shut Down

Like Tara, maybe you shut down in the face of conflict. Your good
intentions, to avoid confrontation, can be useful in situations
where you're too upset to have a productive conversation. However, when you avoid conflict at any cost, your behavior goes beyond

simply avoiding things when you're too upset; you become incommunicative, which allows situations to fester, making them worse, not better. The typical outcome is that the conflict is prolonged in "simmer mode." It remains unaddressed until it eventually breaks out again, sometimes more intensely than before.

Alexandra and Jayson worked together at a global law firm. When they were finishing a meal with some friends at the company cafeteria one day, Alexandra casually asked Jayson if she could transfer one of his star associates onto her team since she had a huge case coming up that would require the best talent at the firm.

Jayson demurred, avoiding the question. He felt miffed. The associate in question was already working on a tough, important case and it bothered him that Alexandra seemed to assume that her project was more important than his own. Jayson knew he'd have to say no, but he was already late to his next meeting and didn't have time to get into a heated debate right there in the cafeteria.

When Alexandra emailed Jayson a week later saying she really needed the associate and asked again if it was okay to make the transfer, Jayson didn't have time to respond to the email. He was too busy with casework.

When Jayson got another email from Alexandra the following week saying that if she didn't hear from Jayson by the end of the day, she would let the associate know about the switch, Jayson went into crisis mode. He had to put all his casework on hold while he dealt with Alexandra's threat.

Shame Yourself

Unlike Javier, who blamed Tara for what he saw as her mistake, you may blame yourself when you're in conflict. When you take the blame, your well-intentioned goal is to learn and do better next time. The upside is that you're taking responsibility for your own actions and you're focused on how you can improve. But when you're compelled to do this regardless of the extent to which you played a part in any particular situation, and when you feel that not only did you *do* something wrong but you *are* bad or wrong, your original intention to learn becomes distorted. Though you may extract some helpful lessons, your learning is overshadowed by shame. The conflict is prolonged while you put yourself through the wringer unnecessarily.

When Marcus's boss told him that his lack of knowledge about a client's business had put their company into a tough spot at a client meeting, Marcus immediately let his boss know that he would learn whatever was needed so this wouldn't happen again. Inside, he felt deeply ashamed about his lack of knowledge and blamed himself for how poorly the meeting had gone. Later that night, alone in his bed, he told himself, "My boss is right. I don't know anything about the client's business. I'd better go back to school and get a real degree. I should've known I didn't have what it takes to be successful here. Who was I kidding? I can't believe I was so stupid . . ." His desire to improve was helpful, but blaming and shaming himself by stewing in negative self-talk reduced the odds that he would do better in the future. All that negativity distracted him from learning and only kept him stuck in conflict while the wheels of his mind spun around and around.

Relentlessly Collaborate

When faced with conflict, you may seek to collaborate with others. Your goal is to resolve conflict amicably. Sometimes you're able to do this, as when you and your colleagues are trying to solve a problem and each of you has functional knowledge the others can benefit from. You share expertise, brainstorm options, and solve the problem. But often, because of unaddressed, deeply held values and emotions, one or more people are not prepared to collaborate.

Although it may not seem so on the surface, particularly because collaboration is so highly prized in our culture, your seeking to collaborate in such circumstances can be just as counterproductive as engaging in any of the other conflict habits.

When you're relentlessly collaborative, your well-intentioned openness to others becomes warped. You're on a mission to collaborate at any cost. You end up wasting valuable time and energy devising potential solutions that will *never* satisfy the others involved.

Either you reach a "Band-Aid" solution that unravels later, or things escalate into a more heated dispute, all while time continues to tick by. This happens in the international sphere, where diplomatic leaders spend years trying to collaborate with others who have no interest in doing so, and it also happens in more common interactions.

After eighteen months as a top-performing account executive at Javier's prestigious design firm, Akiko had her sights set on becoming chief operating officer, a position that had recently become vacant. Javier agreed that Akiko was the best fit for it. However, on a few occasions, Tara and Javier had already had informal conversations that had led Tara to assume that *she* would be offered the role, which would represent a significant promotion for her in terms of both responsibility and stature.

When Javier offered the role to Akiko, Tara was furious and threatened to quit. Since Tara was already a key member of the team and also a good friend of Javier's, he didn't want to lose her. He told Akiko and Tara that it was up to them to see if they could share the role. Akiko had been trained in conflict resolution skills, and that, along with her collaborative nature, led her to try to work it out with Tara.

For many months, Akiko developed option after option with Tara. Tara would entertain each idea but ultimately reject it. The more time that went by, the more frustrated Akiko became. After several months of conversation, Tara continued to refuse all the options. The chief operating officer role was still vacant, and the relationship between Akiko and Tara had deteriorated badly.

Understand Your Own Conflict Habits

Self-knowledge is power, and understanding your conflict habits will loosen their grip on you. Review the four descriptions. Which one might be your primary habit? Although you may use different habits depending on whether you are at work, at home, or in the community, it is still useful to ask yourself which habit you use *most* often.

If that's hard to answer, consider this: Which habit feels most *comfortable* or *alluring* to you? Remember, you use each habit with good intentions. So be honest. You're not doing anyone any good by identifying someone else's habit. Knowing yourself is the first step toward freedom.

Javier, the CEO of the design firm, certainly wasn't happy to admit it, but he knew that his modus operandi was to yell at people when they didn't do what he wanted. Interestingly, he thought he did this more at work than at home. His fiancée was the closest person in the world to him. She understood him and helped him as much as he helped her. At work, people were always angering him by telling him bad news, interrupting him, and doing things badly or completely wrong. It was easy to fly off the handle when he was surrounded by difficult people all day long. But if he was really honest with himself, he could admit that whether at home or at work, when he got upset, Blame Others was his default.

Notice Conflict Patterns

You can't know for sure what other people's primary habits are unless you ask them, but it can be helpful to make your best guess.

Your purpose is not to judge or label other people; your purpose is to understand how you and they have gotten stuck.

Once you identify other people's primary conflict habits, you'll notice a pattern, which is simply the interaction between your conflict habit and theirs.

Here are the five most common conflict patterns I've come across in my work.

The Blame/Shame Pattern

One of my students, Anjali, felt constantly chastised by her aunt for never being good enough—not a good enough daughter, niece, student, friend, cousin, soccer player, scientist, and the list went on. Each time her aunt attacked her for not being good enough at something, Anjali continued her aunt's tirade inside her own head. If her aunt told her she wasn't a good friend, Anjali thought about all the ways she had let her friends down over the years. If her aunt said she wasn't a good enough soccer player, Anjali piled on the criticism, recalling every goal she had ever missed. Anjali and her aunt were a perfect pair—if she wanted to torment herself by keeping count of all the ways she didn't measure up!

The Blame/Shut Down Pattern

Tara noticed that Javier's primary conflict habit seemed to be Blame Others, while her own was Shut Down. She wondered whether that might at least partially explain why their interactions often seemed to go nowhere. Javier would get angry and explode in a fit of rage, which would send Tara heading for the door, and she would stay away until she was sure Javier had calmed down, sometimes days or weeks later. That pattern wasted time that could have been spent in creative pursuits but instead was lost to the dynamic of Javier's exploding and Tara's hiding.

The Relentlessly Collaborate/Shut Down Pattern

For her part, Akiko was able to see how her desire to collaborate was leading nowhere. She and Tara were in a pattern where Akiko would make overtures and Tara would rebuff them. When Akiko was finally able to admit "defeat," she didn't know what should come next, but she did know that more collaborative effort wasn't likely to free her or anyone else from their situation.

The Shut Down/Shut Down Pattern

Jasmine and her sister Theresa hadn't talked to each other in years. It started after their mother had passed away, when they'd had a big blowup about how to divide her belongings. After they had left their mother's house for the last time, neither one of them had picked up the phone to call the other, not even on birthdays or holidays. They had never gotten along well, and now that their mother was gone, there was even less reason to work things out (except for the sake of their children, who hadn't done anything wrong).

The Blame/Blame Pattern

Javier identified his father's primary conflict habit as Blame Others. That helped him understand why he and his father so easily got into fights about everything: whenever either of them went on the attack, the other one attacked back. That created a conflict pattern that seemed impossible to escape.

Notice Groupwide Conflict Habits and Patterns

Like Javier and his father, you may find that you share a conflict habit with someone else or even with a whole group of people. In fact, it is not uncommon for people with similar backgrounds, skills, or traits—whether family history, cultural expectations, personality characteristics, or professional expertise—to share the same conflict habit.

Andre, a human resources executive at a global media firm, was struggling with the leaders of the company's advertising sales team. When Andre sent an email to the three leaders of the team to request that they abide by a new company policy, they outright refused, replying to his email in ways that he perceived to be belligerent.

That went on for a few months as Andre made a series of requests to the advertising sales leaders that were rejected. Eventually the situation deteriorated to the point where Andre was no longer on speaking terms with the three leaders, and he was at a complete loss for what to do next.

When Andre learned the Optimal Outcomes Method as a student in my course at around that time, he challenged himself to try to identify the sales leaders' conflict habits. He thought they exhibited Blame Others. That made sense when he stopped to think about it. In order for the sales leaders to be successful at their jobs, they needed to be good at building relationships with their customers. But particularly in their newly consolidated marketplace, first and foremost, they needed to win market share by beating the sales teams from other firms in their space.

Andre realized that the sales leaders' work required them to be competitive. In addition, he noticed that the culture of the sales team reflected a competitive spirit, as evidenced by their ambitious team motto, "Triple sales or go home."

Andre saw that although the sales leaders' competitive spirit might have helped them do critical aspects of their jobs successfully, when their competitive spirit went into overdrive, it may also have led him to feel blamed and attacked. And the fact that all three leaders were attacking him at once had overwhelmed him.

After identifying the sales leaders' habit as Blame Others, Andre asked himself what the conflict pattern between himself and them was. To his surprise, he was able to admit that he shared their conflict habit. When the sales team perceived his initial request as an attack on them, their own attack impulses were activated. He knew they were stuck in a Blame/Blame conflict pattern.

Andre noticed a pattern of interaction between himself and a group. But conflict patterns exist at every level: between and among individuals, groups, teams, organizations, communities, and even entire countries.

What *Not* to Do

Starting in 2003, a popular reality television show called *What Not to Wear* aired on the TLC network, hosted by Stacy London and Clinton Kelly. Stacy and Clinton pledged "to rescue the frumpy and dumpy, the mismatched and ill-flattered, and give them a life-changing fashion makeover."

Before Stacy and Clinton took people shopping for new clothes, they examined their existing outfits and identified what they should no longer wear. Stacy would pick up articles of clothing and proclaim them off limits: "No more baggy sweatpants; get those out of here!" "Send those ripped T-shirts to the garbage bin!" The person to whom the clothes belonged would chuckle with a tinge of embarrassment, look longingly at the ones that were no longer fit to wear, and place them in the giveaway pile. Only once the person was willing to look honestly at the old clothes and remove them from the closet did it make sense to shop for new clothes.

Similarly, at this stage, you are coming face to face with what *not* to do when you are in conflict. Returning to my personal story for a moment, I could see that avoiding my mom's calls had gotten me into even more trouble than answering them with an impatient, irritated attitude. But both responses accelerated our journey around the conflict loop.

The most effective way to interrupt an old habit is to replace it with something radically different. For example, scientific research by Dr. Wendy Wood, as popularized by Charles Duhigg's bestselling book *The Power of Habit: Why We Do What We Do in Life and Business* suggests that the way to change a bad habit is to replace it with a different habit that will get you the outcome you're seeking. The practices in part III of this book will help you replace your old conflict habit with something different—something pattern breaking—that will help you achieve an Optimal Outcome.

However, as the research shows, before you can replace a bad habit with a different one, you need to become aware of what you've been doing. In order to make a change, the first practice is to raise your awareness of what your habits and patterns have been.

Acknowledge What Is

With the help of my class, I began to see that my mother and I were locked in a Blame/Blame pattern that often ended when I eventually Shut Down. Coming to that conclusion didn't flood me with the hope and motivation that sometimes follows a revelation. Instead, I felt sad. My mother and I loved each other, I knew that, yet we seemed programmed to mistreat each other. And as I began to notice the same conflict pattern bubbling up in other parts of my life—with my family, primarily, but also sometimes with friends, neighbors, and colleagues—I felt overwhelmed.

Fortunately, I had already helped so many people through the process that I knew the stage I was in, though uncomfortable, was both temporary and necessary.

Once you become aware of what your primary conflict habit is, you may begin to notice yourself doing it in your daily life. As you catch yourself engaging in your habit, it might seem as if your actions are happening in slow motion or you're watching yourself on a movie screen.

When this happens, you may feel a sense of relief. You may be ready to leave your old habit behind, and you know that the better you can see it, the greater capacity you have to let it go.

But if you're like me and many other people, you may feel disappointed, both about your habit and about the patterns you're in with other people. For example, maybe you wish your partner wasn't so frustratingly competitive or that you didn't fall into the damn Shut Down habit every single time.

This is normal. When in conflict, we tend to make the same three wishes: we wish the situation would just go away; we wish other people were different from how they are; and many of us (especially those whose primary habit is Shame Yourself) wish we ourselves were different! When our wishes don't match reality, we can feel frustrated and disappointed, mad and sad.

Though wishing things to be different may be human nature and can stimulate positive change when channeled appropriately, these wishes often stand in the way.

For example, wishing a situation would disappear only allows it to continue to brew.

Expecting other people to change simply because you want them to often provokes them. This is due in part to what psychologists call the phenomenon of self-threat. Because humans have an innate need to maintain a positive view of ourselves, we tend to be threatened by, and therefore ignore, reject, or become defensive or even aggressive, in reaction to information that does not confirm this view. When you want someone else to change, this can threaten their positive view of themselves, which means they are not likely to budge and may even become provoked.

And wishing you yourself were different doesn't actually create real change.

As Ray Dalio, founder of the iconic hedge fund Bridgewater Associates, wrote, "People who confuse what they wish were true with what is really true create distorted pictures of reality that make it impossible for them to make the best choices."

In Practice 8, we'll come back to wishing and what to do about it, including how to assess reality and take it into account. For now, simply take a moment to pause and reflect on what you have noticed.

Let's begin now.

Take a deep breath.

Notice the air coming in as you breathe in and going out as you breathe out.

You can do this as few or as many times as you like.

When you're ready, consider the following questions:

* How would you describe your primary conflict habit?

* Thinking about the situation you identified at the end of the introduction, how would you characterize one other person's (or group's) primary conflict habit?

* Has that person or group's conflict habit been interacting with your own conflict habit to form a pattern? If so, which one?

See if you can let whatever you've noticed be what it is. There's no need to change or do anything about it yet.

Just notice.

Chapter Summary

* We try, but typically fail, to resolve recurring conflicts through the use of four conflict habits: Blame Others, Shut Down, Shame Yourself, and Relentlessly Collaborate.

* Each conflict habit interacts with each of the other three, and with itself, to create conflict patterns that keep us stuck in the conflict loop.

* The first practice to free yourself from conflict is to simply notice your primary conflict habit and the conflict pattern to which your habit is contributing.

Apply the Practice

NOTICE YOUR CONFLICT HABITS AND PATTERNS

Identify Your Habit

Of the four conflict habits, which is your primary one?

* Blame Others
* Shut Down
* Shame Yourself
* Relentlessly Collaborate

Identify the Pattern

Of the five most common conflict patterns, which, if any, are you involved in with others?

* The Blame/Shame pattern
* The Blame/Shut Down pattern
* The Relentlessly Collaborate/Shut Down pattern
* The Shut Down/Shut Down pattern
* The Blame/Blame pattern

Notice

Simply notice the habit and pattern you've identified. There is no need to change or do anything about them yet.

You can take an online assessment to identify
your primary conflict habit at:
optimaloutcomesbook.com/assessment

How to Achieve an Optimal Outcome

PART I	UNDERSTANDING THE CONFLICT LOOP
Practice 1	Notice Your Conflict Habits and Patterns
PART II	BREAKING THE CONFLICT PATTERN
PART III	FREEING YOURSELF FROM THE LOOP

PART II

Breaking the
Conflict Pattern

❋

Increase Clarity and Complexity: Map Out the Conflict

For the simplicity on this side of complexity, I wouldn't give you a fig. But for the simplicity on the other side of complexity, for that I would give you anything I have.

—OLIVER WENDELL HOLMES, JR.

The first time I met my client Bob, I was impressed by him and intrigued by his leadership challenges. He was a smart, thoughtful guy with dirty blond hair and a warm smile. He was struggling to take his business to the next level. He was particularly perplexed by how to handle a tough interpersonal issue with someone on his team. He had come to me through a referral from an executive coach who had been working with him for months without making progress. She felt that she was in over her head, and, knowing that my expertise was irreconcilable differences, she thought I could help Bob before he self-destructed.

Bob was the founder of an agile software company that he had started from scratch a decade before. He had enjoyed building the company but was eager to move on to something new and was starting to think about his eventual exit. He had hired a new, more experienced chief financial officer to help him prepare the company for sale. Among the CFO's first recommendations had been renegotiating the compensation of the company's top salesperson, Sally, who had grown the company with Bob since the early days. In addition to being colleagues, they were friends, constantly on sales calls together, wining and dining clients across the country. All those adventures together had enabled the development of a real friendship over the years.

The CFO had pointed out that Sally was receiving bonuses out of proportion to those paid to the rest of the executives and significantly above market rates. Bob knew it was because her bonus structure had been negotiated years before, when her job had been harder, but now that the company had a stronger reputation, she could work much less and still make the highest commissions. Revising her package made financial sense and was important to improving the company's balance sheet. Bob thought this was reasonable and that Sally should take one for the team. But sensing that she might be unhappy about it, he had decided to start the conversation by email, thinking that this might make things easier. But Sally had ignored the emails. When he had finally tried bringing it up in person, he had dropped it on her as a fait accompli. She had been shocked and angry, yelling at him for even suggesting such a change, and then had stomped away angrily when things had gotten too heated. Every time Bob summoned the courage to bring it up, a similar short exchange repeated itself.

One day, Bob brought up the issue again as they were on their way out of a restaurant from a client lunch. "Sally, we really need to take a look at your compensation package. You know that your bonus structure is way higher than market rates, and we need to bring it down. We've got to get things around here in shape."

"Bob, I've already told you, I don't want to talk about it. We've had this fight so many times. We can talk about anything else but not this, not right now."

Bob raised his voice. "Sally, stop being unreasonable. This is ridiculous. We need to—"

Sally cut in, "How can you call *me* unreasonable? Look who's talking!"

Now they were engaged in a screaming match in the middle of the street, steps from where they had lunched with their client.

"Sally, don't yell at me! What makes you think you can scream at me like I'm a child? I'm your boss!"

"I'm treating *you* like a child? You're the one who decided to bring up my compensation on a street corner, for heaven's sake! Stop yelling at me. This is not the time or place to talk about this!"

"Okay, you know what? You're right. You're always right. Forget about it. Forget I ever said anything!"

With that, Bob turned on his heel and walked in the opposite direction, returning to the office separately from Sally.

When I first met Bob, months had gone by. Not only had Bob failed to raise the issue of Sally's compensation again, they were barely talking, bringing any planning about their business to a grinding halt. Now he was seriously considering firing her—which he knew was a major business risk, because she might take her client relationships with her. He also cared about their friendship and really didn't want the relationship to end. But he was at a loss as to how to bring up Sally's compensation without getting into a fight.

Luckily, he didn't have to, not right away, at least; that part would come later.

Before Bob even thought about taking action, I helped him counterintuitively not *do* anything at all; I helped him simply *observe*. For most people, observing a situation from a bird's-eye view itself is a pattern-breaking experience. As was true for Bob, many of us are so used to scurrying around trying to do something to make the conflict go away that simply observing it without immediately taking action inherently breaks the conflict pattern of the past. As the bestselling Jewish-Buddhist teacher Sylvia Boorstein's humorous book title reminds us: "Don't just do something, sit there."

When we do, we usually notice that the situation is more complex than we originally thought.

Going from Simple to Complex

Conflicts are typically caused by multiple factors, but our tendency is to view the situation in much simpler terms. This inclination to simplify into narrow "us-versus-them" affairs stems from the fight-or-flight instinct, which restricts our focus in the face of danger. When a tiger is charging you, the tiger is all you can afford to pay attention to. Even if you understand that a situation is complicated, your mind seeks rapid clarity so you can take quick action.

For example, when Bob first told me about the situation with Sally, he told me about their fight on the street corner and didn't mention anyone else besides himself and Sally.

We often start by describing conflict situations this way. Turn back to the end of the introduction, where I asked you who was involved in the conflict situation you chose. What did you write down? Did you write the names of only a couple of people or groups? If so, that's probably because of our tendency to boil complex situations down to their simplest terms.

That is why it can be so powerful to do the opposite.

When you take a step back and use a wide-angle lens, you gain a more complex and nuanced understanding of a situation that previously seemed black and white. This allows you to identify levers for change that were impossible to see before and develop approaches to the conflict that are different from when you were looking at the situation in a simpler way. One of the best ways to widen your perspective is to map out the conflict.

I first learned about conflict mapping from my graduate adviser, Dr. Peter T. Coleman, director of the Morton Deutsch International Center for Cooperation and Conflict Resolution at Columbia and founder of the Advanced Consortium on Cooperation, Conflict, and Complexity at Columbia University's Earth Institute. This chapter's practice draws from his research on conflict and dynamical systems.

When I helped Bob create his map, I asked him to begin by identifying as many individuals, groups, and other factors that might be relevant to the situation as he could and to draw circles representing them. I suggested he put people and factors on the map regardless of whether they existed in the past, present, or potentially in the future, whether he knew the people well or not, and whether he was certain of the factors' influence or not. Anything he thought *might* be a factor would be helpful to note at this stage.

I suggested he use each circle to represent one person or a pair, group, team, or entire organization and that he consider which circles belonged inside others. He drew a circle representing himself inside a larger circle called "Exec Team" and a circle representing Sally inside a larger circle called "Sales Team."

Then he enclosed all four circles inside a larger circle called "The Organization" to show that he and Sally were each part of two different teams inside one company. He drew a circle called "VC Investors" half inside and half outside the circle called "The Organization" to indicate that the company's venture capital investors were influential inside the organization but also had responsibilities outside it.

When Bob thought about the factors that influenced how he and Sally had been interacting, he noted their backgrounds: how they had each been raised and their families of origin. Bob knew about Sally's family because, over the course of a decade of friendship, she'd told him stories about her childhood, and he'd even met her dad once or twice when he'd been in town visiting.

You may not know the backgrounds of the people in your own situation, and it's not necessary that you do. But you may know more than you realize. It can be helpful to pause and think about what you *do* know about them. What stories have they told you about how they grew up? Have they told you about their parents? Siblings? Teachers, mentors, or coaches who've had an impact on their lives?

Based on what he'd noticed, Bob drew two circles representing their respective backgrounds and families outside the organization to illustrate that those factors influenced the organization but originally existed outside its structure. He drew lines between the circles to show how they were connected to one another. He added arrows to note the directions of influence between people and factors. He drew a double line to show a strong relationship between himself and Sally. He drew arrows pointing from the VC investors and CFO toward himself to note the pressure he felt to lower Sally's compensation. He drew an X between himself and Sally to note the conflict in their relationship, and he drew a heart on the line connecting Sally to her family since he sensed that she had a deep affection for her family and how she had grown up.

Bob's map looked like this:

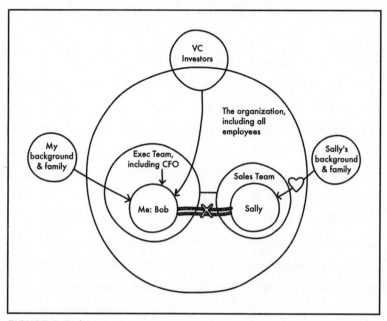

FIGURE 2: Bob's map.

Drawing the map helped Bob gain a more complex view of the situation. He could now see that his conflict with Sally was not just about the two of them but also involved his executive team and in particular the CFO and VC investors, who had advised him that Sally's compensation had to be renegotiated. Indirectly, it also involved the sales team and everyone else at the company, since he knew he had an obligation to act as a strong, fair leader in the company's best interest. It also involved Bob's and Sally's backgrounds, because their life experiences influenced how they thought about compensation and leadership.

Increasing your perception of complexity when things seem black and white is a critical step to help open up a situation that appears hopeless. It raises your awareness of new levers for change.

You can shrink back down to a simpler view of the situation later. But when you begin a process of reflection, complexify.

Going from Fuzzy to Clear

Sometimes the primary benefit of mapping the conflict is that it broadens your perspective, as Bob's map did. Other times, the benefit is the exact opposite: mapping clarifies, even crystallizes, your perspective. If, as you start mapping, you notice that the sheer number of people involved is dizzying, you may realize that one reason the situation has been so difficult is that it seems like a huge, unmanageable mess.

In this case, mapping out the conflict can help you shine a spotlight on the most critical people, groups, and issues at play or help you decide to focus on only one aspect of a much larger situation. It enables you to make a thoughtful choice about where to direct your attention.

If your situation seems overwhelmingly complex, first ask yourself where the "hot spots" are. Who has been most *directly* involved in the conflict? Which issues have been the thorniest? Then ask yourself where the most leverage for change might come from. Who has the potential to be a voice of reason or helpfulness, whether by personality, training, or role? This can help you narrow your focus to the people who are closest to the source of the problem and to the people who can influence dynamics for the better.

If you're dealing with a situation with more hot spots than you can count, ask yourself which part of the situation you want to sink your teeth into, based on your own interests or desire. For instance, if you're dealing with a complex international conflict, you may need to decide whether you are going to work with governmental leaders, grassroots leaders, average citizens representing one, two, or many perspectives in the situation, or the staff of international peacekeeping NGOs. In a situation like this, the possibilities for intervention may seem endless. Mapping can be an effective tool to help you focus your attention.

Finally, mapping can help you define your own role in the situation. Ask yourself, "Am I part of the conflict, or am I a neutral observer in someone else's conflict?" Be aware that in a complex situation where this question seems even the least bit relevant, it is quite possible that you have (or might in the future have) both a direct role in the conflict and a neutral role of sorts.

For example, in family situations, many of my students have discovered that although they have been thinking of themselves as a mediator in a recurring conflict between their parents, they are also part of the conflict simply by virtue of being their parents' child. The reverse also happens: students who think of themselves as being involved in a family conflict suddenly recognize that they have also been playing, and can continue to play, a helpful mediator-type role. And still others realize they have been playing a mediator role in the family that is not healthy and decide that they would rather take a less active role in the situation.

It is important to be aware of any implications of your being directly involved in a conflict situation and taking a neutral role within it. Ask yourself, "How have I been a participant in this situation already? And how have I played a neutral role? Can I imagine playing one or both of these roles in the future? If so, which role(s)? And what might happen if I do that?" (You'll have much more opportunity to think about these questions in part III of the book, but it can be helpful to start thinking about them now.)

When my student Emmanuel began the mapping practice, he was in a state best described as befuddled bewilderment. The idea that he would need to write down the names of dozens of people across three generations of his family, who were dispersed across the United States and Haiti, was overwhelming to him.

When I suggested that he didn't need to name each person individually but could draw circles showing groups of family members, he decided to give it a try. After a few frustrating attempts, he finally hit on something he hadn't noticed before: when he had the courage (or audacity, as he saw it) to put himself at the center of his map, everything else started falling into place. He drew lines representing his relationships with his parents and his grandparents, as well as with each of his aunts, uncles, and first cousins.

Emmanuel also decided to put the United States and Haiti on his map, which helped him become aware of his inner conflict about his dual allegiances to his modern life in the United States and his spiritual life in Haiti. He was engaged to be married to an American woman, and he was studying and planning to become a psychologist in Boston, so he had firm commitments to stay in the United States. But he also had spiritual and familial ties to his traditional life in Haiti, where he was expected to assume his grandmother's position in the community.

This is Emmanuel's map and key:

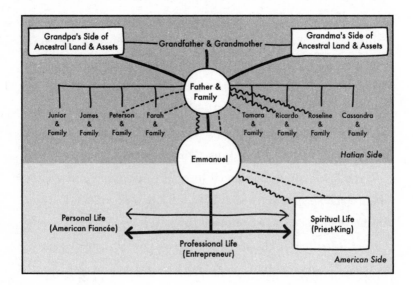

———————————— For my father, connections between all siblings. For me, connections in my American life.

☐ + ◯ People, assets, and factors that are instrumental to my successfully being initiated into my role.

- - - - - - - - - - - Damaged relationships defined by aggression, authority, and control.

〰〰〰〰〰 Shaky relationships defined by gossip, drama, and confrontation.
Can turn to - - - at any point.

━━━━━━━━━ Direct inheritance, oversight, and management of land and spiritual assets.

▓▓▓ The contrast of my two worlds: the Haitian side, defined by tradition, family, and community, and the American side, defined by progress and achievement of personal dreams.

FIGURE 3: Emmanuel's map and key.

Notice What Your Map Tells You

Once you've drawn your map, it's time to pause and observe it. As soon as Emmanuel looked at his finished map, he saw clarity in a situation that had overwhelmed him only minutes before. He knew that his parents understood that he was expected to succeed his grandmother as the next chosen spiritual leader in the lineage of their ancestors, according to Haitian tradition. However, his relationships with his extended family and, in particular, with several aunts, uncles, and cousins had become strained as a result of their own bids to become heir to this seat.

Though Emmanuel had accepted the notion that he would be first in the lineage to receive the honor, when he was honest with himself, he was also terrified of assuming the responsibility.

He was able to see that his ambivalence about succeeding his grandmother had contributed to the conflicts he was experiencing with his relatives. During the years it had taken him to come to terms with his responsibility as an heir to his grandmother's priesthood, his relatives had taken steps to assume the role themselves. His ambivalence due to fears of physical and spiritual safety, which had led him to hesitate to take action, had left an open space for these conflicts to arise. Noticing this produced a helpful "Aha!"

moment for Emmanuel. Now that he understood how he himself had contributed to the family's conflict dynamics, he had the power to clarify his intentions and, in so doing, to improve a situation that had previously felt out of his control.

Let's return to Bob's situation and see what he noticed. Looking at his map, Bob was able to see that pressure from the company's VC investors and CFO had left him feeling stuck between them and Sally. On the one hand, as Sally's friend, he wanted to protect her from their scrutiny and business-comes-first attitude. On the other hand, Sally's unwillingness to even talk about her compensation left Bob feeling disrespected and pushed away, not exactly leading him to want to lend her a helping hand.

This more complex and nuanced picture of the situation gave Bob a sense of empathy; he was able to see himself and Sally as part of a wider system with many influences at play. With this new perspective, he couldn't in good conscience keep pointing his finger only at Sally when he knew all these other forces also had an effect.

Bob's map also brought into clearer focus the impact that Sally's upbringing might be having on her today. He had long known that Sally had grown up in a family where money was scarce. However, it hadn't occurred to him that because of this, she might still be fearful that she wouldn't have enough, even if that was no longer a logical concern. He wasn't sure that was the case, but it did seem plausible. And he was able to appreciate that as a single person without a family to fall back on financially, she knew she would have no one to help her if she faltered. He could see that she probably felt more pressure to keep her finances stable than he had initially realized. Though he still found her behavior infuriating, he could at least now understand where it might originate from, which led him to feel more empathetic toward her.

Finally, Bob noticed that his own background had influenced his ideas about leadership. His father and older brother were both entrepreneurs and had encouraged him to take risks at an early age to follow his passion for technology. He had embraced it, cofounding a small, agile software company with friends during college and living in a communal house with those same buddies. The agile space in general, the company in particular, and the communal house had all been known and prized for their collaborative ethos. Many years later, Bob was still not totally comfortable with the decision-making authority that his role as CEO conferred upon him. Though he knew he technically had the authority to change Sally's compensation, something about that type of authority didn't feel right to him and led him to waver about whether and how to make the change. Though it wasn't easy to admit it, he could acknowledge that his own ambivalence about decision making might be playing a role in getting them stuck.

Bob began to see that the problem wasn't just "over there" with Sally. He could take ownership of parts of it. And as he did so, he began to understand that he had more leverage to change the situation than he had originally thought. He started to consider his own behavior and how he could change it to get the results he was looking for.

Map Your Situation

We will return to Bob and Sally's situation throughout the book. For now, it's your turn to create a conflict map. In the middle of a large blank page, write down the names of the people or groups you identified at the end of the introduction.

Now your job is to add as many people, places, events, ideas, and other factors to the map as you can. Pay particular attention to include people, places, events, ideas, and other factors that might not have been obvious to you before. They can be factors from the past, that are occurring today, or that you anticipate may influence the situation in the future.

Then draw circles and lines to show how all the factors are connected.

Be sure to put *at least* one new person or aspect of the situation on your map that you didn't consider relevant before. Draw or write anything on your map that will help you understand the situation better. For example, thick arrows can denote exertion of pressure or influence or simply strong relationships. You can use different colors to represent the feelings you get from different people or groups of people. Or you can add shapes, colors, pictures, or words inside each circle to represent the meaning a person, place, event, idea, or factor holds for you. An icon or image on a line between circles might show the quality of the relationships between people.

Be creative. Your map should tell the story of the situation in a different way than you have told it in the past. (Don't worry if your map gets messy; the messiness may be an accurate reflection of the reality of the situation, and it can be helpful to see it written down.)

Now take a look at your map. What story does it tell? Is this story different from your original description of the conflict at the end of the introduction? If so, how?

I hope that mapping your situation gives you some new insight, at least enough to create even a small break in the conflict loop. Building on this, the next chapter will help you see how emotions—both your own and others'—have contributed to the situation and how you can use emotions to continue to break the conflict loop.

Chapter Summary

* Conflicts are typically caused by multiple factors, but our tendency is to view situations in much simpler terms. This may help us in a fight-or-flight situation, but it is not helpful when we seek to understand the sources of recurring conflict.

* When you take a step back and use a wide-angle lens, you gain a more complex and nuanced understanding of a situation that previously seemed black and white. This allows you to identify levers for change that were impossible to see before and develop approaches to the conflict that are different than if you were still looking at the situation in a simpler way.

* One of the best ways to widen your perspective is to map out the conflict. Once you've done so, pause to look at it, and notice what it tells you.

* Sometimes the benefit of mapping a conflict is that it broadens your perspective. Other times, it is the exact opposite: mapping clarifies, even crystallizes, your perspective.

Apply the Practice

INCREASE CLARITY AND COMPLEXITY: MAP OUT THE CONFLICT

* *Sketch.* On a blank page, write down the names of the people or groups from the situation that you identified at the end

of the introduction. Draw circles around the names and lines to show how the people are connected.

* *Add.* Add as many people, places, events, ideas, and other factors to the map as you can. These can be factors from the past, present, and possible future that you think may influence or be influenced by the situation. Be sure to put *at least* one new person or aspect of the situation on your map that you hadn't before considered relevant.

* *Be creative.* Draw or write anything on your map that will help you understand the situation better. Your map should tell the story of the situation in a different way than you have told it in the past.

* *Observe.* Look at your map. What story does it tell? Is this story different from your description of the conflict at the end of the introduction? What do you notice about the conflict now, that you didn't notice before you drew your map?

You can download a worksheet to create your own conflict map at:
optimaloutcomesbook.com/map

✳

Put Your Emotions to Work for You

Our feelings are our most genuine paths to knowledge.

—AUDRE LORDE

In the animated film *Inside Out*, eleven-year old Riley Anderson moves to a new school and is nervous about making new friends. The film shows how Riley's emotions—personified as the characters Joy, Anger, Fear, Sadness, and Disgust—work together to help her navigate the big transition.

The creators of the film consulted the renowned psychologist Dr. Paul Ekman to help choose and represent these emotions accurately. Ekman's research on emotions began in Papua New Guinea in the late 1960s and spanned the globe over the next five decades. In his groundbreaking work, he found that those five emotions—joy, anger, fear, sadness, and disgust—are common to all people regardless of national, ethnic, racial, religious, gender, age, or any other cultural or biological differences. A recent meta-survey of emotions researchers suggests widespread support for the idea that these five emotions are universal.

There are, of course, various states and intensities associated with each of these five emotions. On the phone with my mother, I was always amazed by how easily my annoyance became fury, but it makes a lot of sense when you remember that they are both part of the same continuum, anger. I'd feel annoyed when I picked up the phone, miffed when she told me I hadn't called her in two weeks, then furious when she implied that I was lying to her when I said I was too busy to talk. "I'm not stupid!" she'd shout. "I know you find time to call your friends!"

Just as anger spans from irritation to fury, sadness includes disappointment and anguish; fear covers trepidation and outright terror; disgust ranges from dislike to hatred; and joy incorporates contentment and ecstasy. In addition, we're capable of feeling more than one emotion at once. From those five seemingly simple emotions is woven the rich tapestry of feelings and expression that make being human so wonderfully complex.

Going from Empathy to Self-awareness

In the years since Daniel Goleman awakened the professional world to the importance of emotional intelligence, the zeitgeist has changed accordingly. Empathy and sensitivity to other people's emotional states are now rightly extolled as extraordinarily important business skills, with active listening as a go-to tactic to succeed at both.

But in this chapter, instead of concentrating on how to understand *other* people's emotions, we're going to focus on how you tend to experience and express your *own* emotions. We'll also focus specifically on anger since it plays an outsized role in perpetuating the conflict loop.

You might ask why you need to look at your own emotions when it often seems as though other people's emotions are the problem. This is because, perhaps as a result of the focus in recent years on developing empathy, I've consulted with many people who work so diligently to become attuned to others' emotional states that they end up neglecting their own. The problem is that in order to understand *someone else's* emotional experience, you must first identify and understand *your own*. If you don't, you risk projecting your own emotions onto other people or, equally as problematic, taking on their emotions as if they were your own. Doing either of these things can make it difficult to respond to others in a truly helpful way.

Also, although it may not feel like it in the heat of the moment, you have far more influence over how you experience and express your own emotions than you do over how other people experience and express theirs. The greatest leverage you have for freeing yourself from a tricky emotional dynamic lies in your ability to put your own emotions to work, rather than trying to get someone else to change.

Putting your emotions to work for you does not involve tamping them down, getting rid of them, or scrutinizing why you feel the way you feel. Instead, it includes identifying, acknowledging, and using your emotions as a catalyst for constructive, pattern-breaking action.

Of all the practices you'll learn in the Optimal Outcomes Method, this one is crucial. You simply cannot free yourself from the conflict loop if you are unable to use your own emotions toward constructive change.

Nature and Nurture Influence Our Emotions

When I was a kid, my father got the nickname "Honkin' Hank" because of how often he blasted the car horn to alert other drivers to get out of his way. As I grew up witnessing this behavior from the back seat of the family car (and being my father's daughter), my anger is also triggered easily. When someone cuts me off on the highway, the blood rushes to my face, my heartbeat gets faster, my thinking gets clouded, and if I don't pause before responding, I will blast my car's horn just as my dad did.

Though biology influences how we experience and express our emotions, the messages we receive about how to do so also play a part. For instance, during our formative years, we learn how to experience and express our emotions by watching how our family members, teachers, community leaders, and role models in the culture at large do so. As we get older, we continue to be influenced by others as well as by situational expectations and norms, whether specific to a particular classroom, workplace, or community culture. Nature and nurture together influence how we experience and express our emotions.

Emotional Experience

The experience of an emotion manifests in your body both physically and psychologically and can range from *high intensity* to *low intensity*. For example, a high-intensity emotional experience of anger could involve your body becoming very hot and sweaty and your thoughts focusing on how others are to blame. A low-intensity emotional experience of anger may involve a subtle sensation of tightness in your neck and fleeting thoughts about something that seems unfair to you.

High-Intensity Emotion

Javier, the design company CEO, tends to experience his emotions intensely. When he feels joyful, he feels physically lighter and a large smile comes to his face. He thinks about the circumstances that bring him joy, and tears of happiness roll down his cheeks uncontrollably. When he feels sad, tears also well up in his eyes and flow easily. His voice wavers and gets crackly. His thoughts focus on the events that cause him to feel sad.

Low-Intensity Emotion

In contrast to Javier's high-intensity emotional experiences, when Gerard, the founder of a global biotech start-up, feels angry or joyful or fearful, he notices it, but barely. His physical cues are muted, and he doesn't spend much time thinking about how he feels.

In its extreme form, scientists have found that some people tend to have such low-intensity emotional experiences that their emotions simply don't register at all. When asked, they are not able to name their emotions. This condition often occurs as a result of trauma, which causes people to distance themselves from their emotions to protect themselves from reexperiencing the original pain.

But Gerard doesn't have a history of trauma. He can name his emotions, even if they are muted and even if doing so doesn't come naturally or easily. Like Gerard, many people tend to experience their emotions with low intensity, whether as a result of biological makeup, social norms, traumatic events, or some combination.

Emotional Expression

While we experience our emotions by feeling and thinking about them, we *express* them by *acting on* and *talking about* them. We express our emotions along two dimensions: *level of constructiveness* and *ease of expression*.

Level of Constructiveness

The way you express your emotions can range from highly constructive to highly destructive.

If you feel angry, a constructive response may be to talk with others about the cause of your anger, while a destructive response might be to act violently against others. If you feel sad, a constructive response might be to gather with others to grieve a loss, while a destructive response may be to harm yourself physically. If you feel disgust, a constructive response may be to distance yourself from the person or thing that disgusts you, while a destructive response may be to aggress against the object of your disgust.

Both Javier and Bob tended to express their anger destructively. When either of them received a phone call from an angry client, they would slam the phone down and immediately call the manager at fault. They would speak loudly and in a gruff voice and warn the manager that if the same thing happened again, he'd better start looking for another job. Then they would slam down the phone again.

Ease of Expression

The way you express your emotions can also range from easy to difficult.

In the example above, Javier and Bob each found it quite easy to express their emotions (albeit destructively). You may also find it easy to express your emotions: you may express joy by jumping up and dancing when you feel happy; you may express fear by shrieking at a scary movie; or you may express sadness by spontaneously shedding tears when you think of a loved one who has passed away.

In contrast, Gerard, the founder of the global biotech start-up who experiences his emotions with low intensity, found it difficult to express his emotions. One day, Gerard was interrupted during a staff meeting by a phone call from his sister, Laurene. She told Gerard that their father had just had a heart attack. Despite having a close relationship with his father, Gerard heard the news, took it in, and immediately rejoined the meeting without saying anything about it to his colleagues.

When he finally told his colleagues later that week what had happened to his dad, they were shocked to hear the news. They couldn't believe he had taken the phone call in the hallway and returned as if nothing had happened. But that was typical of Gerard: it is hard for him to express his emotions.

Emotion Traps

Depending on how we experience and express our emotions in any given situation, all of us, at one time or another, become vulnerable to each of three emotion traps. However, we are likely to fall into one of these traps more often than the other two based on our experiences in childhood and the cultural norms we've been surrounded by regarding how to experience and express emotions, including those dictated by gender, nationality, religion, and race.

For example, if you grew up in a home where strong emotions were constantly on display, you may have no trouble experiencing and expressing fear, anger, or joy. But if your family kept quiet about their feelings, you may not notice your own emotions very easily, or you may not feel comfortable letting others know when you feel afraid, angry, or even happy.

As you read about the three emotion traps below, consider which of them you are most likely to fall into.

Knee-Jerk Reaction Trap

When you fall into the Knee-Jerk Reaction Trap, *you express a quick reaction based on your emotional experience*. This reaction is the result of your amygdala hijacking the rest of your brain; sensing danger, you leap to react based on emotional memory, rather than relying on slower, more rational frontal-lobe thinking. For instance, Bob became intensely angry whenever people didn't act the way he thought they should, and he often expressed it immediately in an aggressive way. This typically led others to respond by expressing their emotions in ways that were challenging for Bob, such as when Sally responded to him by attacking him back.

It can be helpful to ask yourself which of the five universal emotions you tend to experience most intensely and express most easily. Of the five emotions, like Bob, I tend to experience and express anger most easily, while you may experience and express joy, or fear, or another emotion most easily.

Inaccessible Emotions Trap

When you fall into the Inaccessible Emotions Trap, your emotions exist inside of you, but *they remain inaccessible to others and often even to yourself*.

For example, because Gerard had trouble accessing his emotions, it was often hard for others to know what he was feeling, and they certainly couldn't help him if they didn't know whether he was worried, sad, angry, or none of the above. Also, with his emotions off limits even to himself, it was difficult for him to show empathy for others, which further contributed to the distance people felt in their relationships with him.

Lurking Emotions Trap

Amelia, a newspaper journalist, tends to experience her emotions intensely. However, as a child, her parents did not approve. Whenever she or her sisters cried, complained, or even expressed joy, they were told, "Children are meant to be seen, not heard."

As an adult, not surprisingly, she finds it difficult to express her emotions directly, even when she is experiencing them with intensity. She experiences her emotions, but she does not admit to experiencing them. When she feels joy, she tends not to smile, and she's the last one to join in on the dance floor. When she feels intense anger, she tries hard to cover it up. Her emotions tend to be *hidden but lurking, lying in wait to emerge.* It is the nature of emotions to be expressed. When we do not consciously express them, they often materialize anyway, in ways we don't intend. Because Amelia does not feel comfortable expressing her emotions directly, she has little control over how they will come out. Especially when she experiences emotions intensely, they do inevitably surface—just not always in ways she'd like.

One day during a reporters' meeting, Amelia became furious at a colleague named David whom she felt was trying to edge her out of a plum job assignment. Without intending it, an expression of contempt spread across her face when she looked at him. When colleagues who had been at the meeting told her that she had seemed angry with David, she vehemently denied it and told them they were wrongly accusing her of having been angry when she wasn't. That caused quite a stir between Amelia and her colleagues.

As Amelia discovered, your lurking emotions can betray you by oozing out even when you try to conceal them, which can lead to miscommunications and conflict with others.

Practice Pausing

In order to stop falling into the emotion traps, it helps to take two types of pauses to slow down and observe your emotions: a proactive pause and a reactive pause.

When you have the presence of mind to notice as you're falling into one of the traps, you have the opportunity to take a reactive pause. Instead of reacting to other people, you simply stop and take a short break. You can do this in your head or out loud. For example, if you've gotten trapped while you're in a conversation with the chair of your board, you might decide that it is most appropriate to take a private, internal pause. You might silently count to ten and breathe slowly to calm yourself down before you speak.

But if you've gotten trapped when you're with a friend, family member, or trusted colleague, you can ask that person to hold on or take a break to ease the pressure.

One of my closest friends, Wendy, is great at doing this. Wendy and I often work on client projects together. Every once in a while, she'll ask me to hold on while we're on the phone. She interrupts herself in order to have a quiet moment to notice what is happening in her body—whether she has tightness in her stomach or a lump in her throat—and what emotions she is experiencing regarding whatever question or decision we might be discussing.

I will admit that when Wendy first started this practice, I wasn't sure why it seemed as though she often got an interrupting call and I had to hang on. Then one day I realized she wasn't answering someone else's call—she was answering her own call!

I am grateful for Wendy's ability to do this. First, it has likely saved us both hours of aggravation since she takes a break to figure out what she really wants to say before she says it. Second, while she takes her pause, I get one, too. The few seconds of silence provide just enough time for me to do my own reflection and to consider the response I want to give. The break helps me contribute in a positive way to our relationship and the outcomes we want to create.

But reactive pausing is not fail-safe. It has a catch, particularly for those of us who tend to fall into the Knee-Jerk Reaction Trap or the Lurking Emotions Trap: the greater the intensity of your emotional experience, the more you can benefit from a pause but the harder it can be to pause in the first place. The intensity of your emotions can be overwhelming, making it very difficult to take a break.

I've personally experienced this many times, especially when I'm angry. My knee-jerk reaction is on constant replay, and I feel powerless to stop it.

After two decades of wrestling with this dilemma along with my clients and students, I have found that it is helpful to proactively pause every day, even—especially—when it doesn't seem necessary.

The more practice you have pausing when you're *not* experiencing challenging emotions or interacting with other people, the easier it will be to pause when you feel challenging emotions rising while you are face-to-face with others. A proactive pause may involve letting your mind wander when you're on the train, taking a solo walk in the park and leaving your phone at home, or sitting quietly for five minutes.

Frequency of practice is more important than duration. A proactive pause can be taken in an instant. I've had an image of a Buddha statue as the "wallpaper" on my computer screen since I first took the photo of it more than fifteen years ago on a trip to Cambodia.

Looking at the Buddha whenever I switch computer applications helps me take a one-second pause to observe my feelings in the midst of a busy day.

Acknowledge Your Emotions

Whether you already have a daily pause practice or you're just getting started, you can use proactive pause time to acknowledge and name your emotions. If you're like most high-achieving professionals, you may benefit from some dedicated training. We're under so much pressure to *do, do, do* that taking time for this kind of quiet reflection can feel like an act of rebellion—and liberation.

I felt that way last summer, when I decided to take a four-day pause in the White Mountains of New Hampshire. I've always taken a quarterly retreat for reflection, but typically for twenty-four or forty-eight hours—the maximum time I felt comfortable stepping away from client and parental responsibilities. Even in that short time frame, I'd sometimes feel the tug of guilt distracting me.

This trip was different. My children were both at sleepaway camp, my husband was all in on a huge project at work, and my clients were either on vacation or feeling as though they should be. Freed from all guilt, I committed myself completely to four days in commune with nature and my emotions. Carrying a thirty-pound pack and a tiny Moleskine journal, I decided to let my emotions evolve with the landscape, naming each one as it arose.

My biggest challenge turned out to be keeping the Moleskine dry, because it rained the entire four days. The weather ranged from drizzle to torrential downpour. Nevertheless, the first and most frequent emotions that surfaced were joy and contentment. I was joyful to be alone; to place a rock on a cairn each time I reached a peak; to breathe the fresh air of a place I had spent many happy weekends in my early twenties.

Later I found my thoughts drifting to my aunt, who had been like a second mother to me before we had lost her and my uncle, both to cancer, ten years apart. Sadness descended upon me. I noticed the feeling and kept on walking. Before long the sad feelings disappeared and contentment returned, only to be followed by panic when I found myself ambling up the sheer face of a cliff under a sky that had possible signs of an impending lightning storm. When I heard a panicked internal voice telling me to turn back, I recognized it as just that—a voice. I told the voice that I heard its message, and I reassured it that I'd keep watching the sky for signs of danger. I walked on.

The lightning storm never came, the panic passed, and the joy returned.

I came away reminded that emotions are as transitory as the weather when we actually stop to experience them. The more we practice acknowledging them—allowing them to bubble up, be recognized, and then float away—the more ease we have even when we're in their grip.

Let Your Emotions Settle

Once you acknowledge your emotions, what should you do?

The well-known Vietnamese Buddhist monk Thich Nhat Hanh offers the metaphor of a muddy glass of water when you're in the desert: You want to drink the water, but it's clouded with mud. What to do?

You let the dirt settle to the bottom, so you can drink the clear water.

It's the same with emotions, Hanh says. Don't try to throw away, change, or examine the muddy emotions—just let them settle, and see what happens. Usually something else more constructive appears in their place.

A few years ago, I put Hanh's suggestion to use in a situation that will probably be familiar to many working parents. My daughter's summer camp had just ended, and school had not yet begun.

My husband and I both needed to be in the city the next day for work, and we had asked a babysitter to spend the day at home with our daughter. But when I texted to confirm with the sitter, she replied that she had not been aware that we needed her and she was not available.

When I read her text, I instantly felt angry. I felt the blood rush to my neck and face and my pulse speed up. I was angry at myself for not being clearer when I had told my husband what day the camp ended. I was angry at my husband for not communicating our needs clearly to the sitter. I was angry at the sitter for not being available and for being curt in her reply.

Since I often feel better and get good ideas while running, I decided to go for a run. I came back still steaming.

Then I recalled Thich Nhat Hanh's advice. I hesitantly sat down on my meditation pillow and didn't do much of anything at all. I just sat there looking at some of the photos I'd set out in the little meditation corner of my bedroom.

Within five minutes, it felt as though a positive spell had been cast over me. I was completely calm. I realized that we were all competent, creative people and would figure something out.

When I got up from my cushion, I picked up my phone to text my husband so we could figure out the next day's schedule together. Instead I found a text from the sitter. It read:

I'm sorry. I read the schedule wrong. I will be there tomorrow.

Now, I'm not saying that every time you let your anger settle, a message will magically appear to make things better. I *am* saying that letting the mud settle may not take as long or be as complicated as it seems.

But I know it's not always easy to let your emotions settle, especially if you're experiencing them with high intensity. What if you've taken a pause and you're still upset? What should you do then?

Ask What Your Emotions Are Trying to Tell You

Get to know your emotions as if they're old friends who have come to visit you.

In the film *Inside Out*, each of the animated characters that embody the five core emotions has a distinct personality, look, and sound.

The character named Anger is big and square, with a flaming red body and a gruff, mean-sounding voice.

Fear is skinny, tall, and light purple with a squeamish, high-pitched, shaky voice.

Sadness is shaped like a large blue ball with round eyelids that droop, and a slow, monotone voice.

What do your emotions look, sound, feel, and even smell like?

As I did on the hiking trail in New Hampshire, try talking to them.

If you feel silly doing this in public, do it inside your head or find a quiet place to be alone and say something like "Hello, fear. What are you trying to tell me?"

Then listen for an answer. (If you have a hard time imagining the look and sound of your emotions, their personalities may come out anyway in their answers.)

Here are some common messages that your emotions may be trying to send you:

Anger says: "This is not right. Something needs to change."

Fear says: "Danger ahead!" (Real or perceived.)

Sadness says: "A loss has occurred."

Disgust says: "This is *not* good."

Joy says: "Wow, this is *great*."

One of the most unexpected, emotionally intense coaching experiences of my career involved a rising workplace star named Briana. She had been sent by her law firm to participate in a leadership development program where I was a coach. Briana was on track to become partner—or had been until a few months before I met her.

My role in the program was to review 360-degree feedback with participants, helping them to evaluate it and create a plan for change. Briana was a high-achieving type A personality who told me she had never had a bad performance review in her life. So it had been a shock when the 360-degree feedback data had come in, showing some pretty significant concerns among her coworkers. They reported a downshift in her focus and drive, reflected in her uncharacteristic sloppiness with details and disengagement during group meetings. Some of the junior employees mentioned having been on the receiving end of a temper that suddenly seemed short and erratic. Many of the 360-degree feedback comments began with "Since Briana came back to work . . ."

When we sat down to discuss the feedback, I asked her what she had "come back" from. She told me a very sad story. She had been anticipating becoming a brand-new mother. Instead, six months earlier, after a long and painful delivery, her child had been stillborn. She had used her planned maternity leave to grieve for her baby, whom she had named Alma. She showed me the ring around her finger, engraved with Alma's name and birth date. She said it was hard for people to understand how intensely bonded she was to her stillborn child, which had made her recovery lonely.

Now that she was back at work, she confessed, her reentry had been unexpectedly rocky. She was doubting her commitment to her firm, even to the practice of law. The work she had once enjoyed felt tedious and shallow. The fact that her frustration sometimes erupted into anger with the people around her—spelled out in black and white in the 360-degree feedback—left her feeling terrible.

"Have I spent all these years of hard work creating the wrong career for myself?" she asked me in frustration, twisting the ring on her finger. She was thinking about leaving the firm and changing industries, or even going back to school.

My gut instinct was that Briana's troubles at work didn't stem from being in the wrong field or at the wrong company; they stemmed from the fact that she had forced herself to return to work at the end of what was supposed to have been a happy period of her life, a maternity leave, but those three months simply hadn't been enough time for her to grieve the huge loss she'd been dealt. Being the hard-charging executive she was, she hadn't acknowledged that she was still grieving, and that maybe she wasn't ready to go back to work yet.

I decided to check this with Briana. "Let me ask you something," I said to her gently. "Was the three months you took off enough time? Did it give you the time you needed to grieve?"

She looked up at me with wide eyes and raised eyebrows. "Nope. Definitely not. But I'm worried I'll never feel okay enough to go back. I mean, I thought by the end of three months I should have it all together. Now it's been six months, and I feel almost as terrible today as I did on the day I delivered Alma. When will it ever get better?"

As we sat there together, I felt sadness rising in the pit of my stomach. I noticed Briana struggling to make sense of her own experience, and I heard her worrying that things would never get better. There was a certain gravitas to the moment between us. Instead of ignoring it or pushing it away, I decided to let it be what it was and to pay attention to it. I knew my job wasn't to try to take away Briana's pain; it was simply to bear witness to it.

That created a light-bulb moment for Briana. She recognized that the depth of her loss was even greater and more painful than she had anticipated or wanted it to be. And in hearing her own answer to my question, she began to give herself the permission to continue to pause and grieve.

Briana heeded the message her emotions were sending her. She asked her manager for additional unpaid time off from work so she could recuperate more fully before returning, and she was granted the time.

That ultimately served not only herself and her family but also her relationships with her colleagues and the firm itself. She decided she didn't need a career reboot at all. Her grief and fatigue, not the work itself, had been undermining her. Feeling renewed, she was able to return a few months later. Within a year, she made partner.

Take Constructive, Pattern-Breaking Action

Once you acknowledge your emotions and listen to what they're trying to tell you, then it's time to take constructive action.

When you feel angry, consider how an American civil rights icon handled anger. Do you think the Reverend Dr. Martin Luther King, Jr., never felt angry?

Or that he wanted to get rid of his anger?

Did he pretend that injustice was not occurring?

Did he act out violently?

No. He did none of the above.

He acknowledged his anger and used it as a catalyst for social change. That broke the patterns of interaction in the United States at the time, when people were expressing their anger about lack of civil rights either violently or not at all. Instead, King took constructive, pattern-breaking action.

He articulated the impact of injustice on his people: "Our civil rights have been violated."

He committed himself to the cause of justice.

And he made a clear request of every American: to treat all people equally.

Though his request has not yet been fully realized, his description of the impact of others' behavior, together with his commitment and request, made a difference. They paved the way for much of the civil rights progress in this country over the past fifty years and counting.

Anger—or any other emotion—is not inherently bad. It's what you do with it that can cause it to become a catalyst for either constructive change or destruction.

It's up to you.

Constructive Change for Nonrevolutionaries

You don't have to be the next Martin Luther King, Jr., to take pattern-breaking action. Remember Gerard, the founder of a biotech start-up who tended to fall into the Inaccessible Emotions Trap? He learned to use his anger for constructive action.

One day Gerard found out that a star performer on his team, Whitney, had been recruited by a competing firm and offered double the salary she had been making. When he first learned the news, he felt a dropping sensation in his stomach. He acknowledged that he felt angry at the founder of the competing firm who had recruited Whitney, whom he knew personally. And he could admit that he felt angry at Whitney for entertaining the offer.

The culture of his start-up team was still being built and was fragile. Beyond feeling worried about losing Whitney's talent, Gerard also knew that if Whitney left, it could put a big dent in the team's morale. If he didn't address it, or if he was perceived as responding passive-aggressively toward Whitney, it could have negative consequences both for him and for the rest of his team— including additional turnover, which he could not afford.

After learning the news, Gerard took a walk outside to consider how to respond. When he returned to the office, he was much more clearheaded and asked to meet with his head of people operations. They worked together over the next couple of days to develop a response to Whitney. Then they made her a counteroffer, which she eventually refused, choosing instead to join the competing firm. Though he was disappointed to be losing Whitney, Gerard crafted a thoughtful email to his team, explaining what had happened and asking for their help to get through this tough moment.

Because Gerard broke the pattern of the past by acknowledging his emotions and taking constructive action based on them (such as noticing his anger and making thoughtful requests of others), although the team lost Whitney, the situation didn't lower morale or result in the additional turnover that Gerard had feared.

Observe (and Don't Hold Yourself Responsible for) Others' Paths

Even if you acknowledge and listen to your emotions and take constructive action, other people aren't necessarily going to be able to do the same for themselves. This is an inevitable part of life. You know it when you see it: Your child throws a tantrum. Your spouse freaks out. Your boss has a fit.

The key to freeing yourself in these types of situations is to understand that although other people's emotional expressions may seem to be directed at you or may be occurring in reaction to something you said or did, they are not *only* about you. In fact, much of the time, other people's emotional expressions are not about you at all.

To respond to others as if their words and actions are primarily about you is to not fully acknowledge that other people's emotional expressions are rooted in their *own* emotion traps, which are born of their history, their cultural, national, and religious backgrounds, and how they were raised.

Even if other people express emotions toward you in a challenging or confrontational way, when you remember that they are simply living out their *own* journey, you can learn to de-escalate the tension.

Locate Others' Emotional Expression Where It Belongs: With Them

The ability to distinguish between emotions that stem from your own experience and emotions that arise from someone else's experience can be a difficult skill to build, but it is crucial. One way to do this is to take a moment to pause when you're with other people who are expressing strong emotions. See if you can acknowledge that they are having an emotional experience that is separate from you. Even if they are expressing certain emotions in reaction to something you have said or done, ultimately, what is happening for them belongs to them. You may choose to be there for them as a listening friend or colleague, but you do not need to take on their emotions as if they are your own. Challenge yourself to let their emotions stay with them, where they belong.

Identify Others' Emotional Expressions

By the very nature of our being human, each of us makes sense of the world based on our own experiences and filters. Since you're not other people, you obviously can't know for certain what their emotional experience is or what their intentions are, but it can be helpful to ask yourself which of the five universal emotions they seem to be expressing. You can pause and make a good guess, based on your observations.

How are they expressing, or not expressing, their emotions? Do they seem to be expressing those emotions constructively or destructively? Are they expressing those emotions with ease or difficulty?

Which of the three emotion traps might they be particularly prone to: the Knee-Jerk Reaction Trap, the Inaccessible Emotions Trap, or the Lurking Emotions Trap? Have they fallen into that trap now? If so, how?

Reroute Others' Emotions Back to Them

As we've noted, you have no way of knowing for sure what other people are experiencing inside. But you can share with them *your* understanding, being careful to use simple, constructive, high-level language that allows room for them to acknowledge whether what you're saying is true or not. If it seems appropriate, you can check with them to see if you got it right. It often helps to make a simple observation and ask a question, such as "Wow, it seems like you're upset. Is that right?" Or "Hmmm. It seems hard for you to express what you're feeling. Is that true?"

Again, only if it seems appropriate, you can encourage others by saying something like "If you're comfortable, I'd love to understand what is happening for you." But please do not feel pressured to do this. Remember, your goal is simply to notice what may be going on for them and to redirect their emotional experience back to them, where it belongs.

Recall Tara, who worked with Javier at the design firm. Through our work together, Tara acknowledged that she and Javier had been engaged in an unhealthy conflict pattern for years. He would get angry, and she would shut down. Sometimes his bouts of anger would leave her hiding out for days, unable to be in the same room with him until she felt ready to do so.

But once Tara learned how to separate herself from Javier's emotional experiences and expressions and to reroute them back to him, she was able to break free from their old conflict pattern. One day, when Javier got angry about an important sales presentation slide deck that didn't meet his expectations, he began to hurl insults at Tara. But this time, instead of hanging her head in shame and slinking out of the room as she usually did, she found the courage to reroute Javier's emotions back where they belonged: with him, not with her.

She said, "Javier, it seems like this has you really fired up. What's going on?"

Tara's response caught Javier off guard—in a good way. Especially since he wasn't used to anyone calling him out on his poor behavior, when Tara did, it stopped him in his tracks. He felt slightly embarrassed, and muttered, "I don't know. The slides just aren't what I expected. We need to redo them."

Now that Javier had come down from his tirade, they were able to figure out how to edit the slides without his intense emotions getting in the way.

Now that we've looked at how emotions contribute to keeping you stuck in the conflict loop and how you can use them in your favor, it's time to explore how your values—the things you really care about in life—have gotten you stuck in the conflict loop and how you can use them to break free from it.

Chapter Summary

* We *experience* our emotions by *thinking* about them and *feeling* them physiologically. Our emotions can range from *high intensity* to *low intensity*.

* We *express* our emotions by *acting on* and *talking about* them. We express emotions along two dimensions: *level of constructiveness* and *ease of expression*.

* Depending on how you experience and express your emotions, you are vulnerable to falling into the Knee-Jerk Reaction Trap, the Inaccessible Emotions Trap, or the Lurking Emotions Trap.

* To stop falling into an emotion trap, *pause* to reflect on your emotional experience. Allow your emotions to settle. Ask

what messages your emotions are trying to send you. Then take constructive, pattern-breaking action based on the messages.

* If other people express emotions in a way that is challenging for you, remember that they are living their own journey. Even if they are reacting to something you said or did, their emotional expression is theirs, not yours.

* By making an observation and asking what is going on for them, you can reroute their emotional expression away from you and back to them, where it belongs.

Apply the Practice

PUT YOUR EMOTIONS TO WORK FOR YOU

* *Pause.* Acknowledge and name your emotions. You can do this proactively on a regular basis and also reactively when you feel emotions rising.

* *Settle.* Let your emotions settle. Get to know your emotions as if they're old friends who have come to visit you. What do your emotions look, sound, feel, and even smell like?

* *Ask.* What messages are your emotions trying to send you?

* *Act.* Based on the messages your emotions are sending you, what constructive action can you take that would be

different from what you have done before—that would break the conflict pattern of the past?

> *You can visit Dr. Paul Ekman's Atlas of Emotions,*
> *supported by the Dalai Lama, to learn more about*
> *the five emotions and the states they contain. It is*
> *the best representation of emotions I've seen:*
> *atlasofemotions.org*

> *You can take an online assessment to*
> *identify your Emotion Trap at:*
> *optimaloutcomesbook.com/assessment*

✳

Honor Ideal and Shadow Values—Yours and Theirs

Everyone carries a shadow, and the less it is embodied in the individual's conscious life, the denser it is. At all counts, it forms an unconscious snag, thwarting our most well-meant intentions.

—CARL JUNG

Most of us understand intuitively that there's more—much more—to ourselves than the image we present to the world. Carl Jung created an entire school of psychology around the notion. He defined the public version of ourselves as the *ego* and then turned his attention to the part we keep hidden, even from ourselves. He called this the *shadow self*. Conflicts between the two, according to Jung, are at the heart of almost every conflict that exists in the outer world. To heal, the shadow self must be allowed to come into the light of consciousness, accepted and heard instead of banished in shame. Jung calls this process *individuation*—and it's very similar to the work we'll be doing in this chapter.

Over the course of a lifetime, each of us develops a unique *values fingerprint*. Unlike our actual fingerprints, our values fingerprint is not fixed. It evolves based on our life experiences and our responses to the values we learn from the people around us.

We learn some values explicitly. If you grew up in a religious home, your parents may have taught you the value of caring for others by quoting the biblical phrase "Love your neighbor as yourself." Or if you played on a sports team, your coach might have taught you the value of endurance by yelling "Keep going!" when you felt ready to give up.

Other values are instilled implicitly, without any discussion. That's how I learned my family's value of frugality. My grandparents fled Nazi Europe as young newlyweds, arriving in New York City without a dime and forced to build a new life from scratch. They learned to pinch every penny and reuse everything from old containers to paper to aluminum foil. They were so thrifty that despite years of low-paying jobs, they managed to contribute to my college education, which allowed me not to worry about student debt. They never once suggested that I be frugal, but I sure got the message.

With implicitly learned values, we may not always be aware of how important they are to us and why. We may also lack clarity about our values because we've pushed some of them out of our consciousness. With a nod to Jung, I call these *shadow values*. Unlike *ideal values*, which we're proud to hold openly, shadow values are hard for us to admit, even to ourselves. Because we're in denial about them, we're often unaware that they are leading us to speak and act in ways that exacerbate conflicts.

But what leads us to cast certain parts of ourselves into the shadow in the first place?

How Values Go Undercover

We push values into the shadow because we've received mixed messages about them. For instance, I attended a public school system in the Bronx that rewarded being highly competitive with other students. In order to get into a good magnet high school, I had to score in the top percentile on a citywide exam at age fourteen, and I was determined to make the cut. Once there, I worked hard, and I relished the highs and managed the lows that fierce competition brought. Years later, shortly after I arrived at a private college in New England, far from the gritty Bronx, an English professor called me aside to tell me that he thought I was being too competitive with the other students in the class. I was mortified. I desperately wanted to fit in, so I began to hide my love of competition. But being competitive was a part of me. I had benefited from competing and knew it had helped me get into my dream schools in the first place.

So what happened? I went undercover with my competitive spirit. In graduate school, I applied for national fellowships without telling any of my friends or colleagues. What's more, if anyone ever suggested that I was competitive, I felt I was being attacked. I was extremely embarrassed, even humiliated. Years later I realized that this is exactly the kind of shadow value that rouses emotion and spills out into conflicts with others.

But the social messaging that leads us to push values into the shadow is often less overt than my professor's flat-out telling me I was too competitive. For example, soon after my colleague Max joined a global firm as a junior consultant, he excitedly asked a much-admired partner he'd accompanied to a meeting with a potential client, "Did we win the business?" The partner replied, "We didn't *win* the business, but we did gain the opportunity to serve." Though the partner didn't exactly say it, Max got the message that it was crude to value selling; the firm valued client service above all else. Afterward, Max did his best to hide his love of making a sale, and if anyone at the firm ever suggested that his client presentations were too sales focused, he felt accused and embarrassed.

One Person's Ideal Is Another Person's Shame

We are typically reluctant to admit to our shadow values because we are ashamed of them. The ironic thing is that shadow values differ widely from person to person, and a value that might seem obviously "good" or ideal to one person can be a shadow value for someone else.

How it is possible that some of us are proud to hold values that others are ashamed of? It is due to differences in social conditioning. Messages about what is okay and not okay are different from home to home, community to community, and organization to organization.

One of my clients, Marcia, cherishes being able to set her own work hours and days, just as her father did. So for her, independence is an ideal value. Another client, Jakob, grew up in a large family with an ethic that everybody should work together to do chores. He learned that the desire for independence was selfish, even though he secretly wants to do his own thing. For him, independence is a shadow value.

Identify Your Ideal Values

To help you break the conflict pattern of the past in whatever situation you're struggling with, you first need to identify your values. If you've never considered what your values are, or if it's been a while, it can be hard to articulate them. The Values Inventory in appendix 1 is by no means comprehensive, but I've found it to be a powerful tool.

This is an emotional exercise as much as an intellectual one. Let your gut be your guide. Looking through the Values Inventory and keeping in mind your conflict situation, put a check mark next to the top ten ideal values that speak to you. Ideal values are simply the things you are proud to say you care about. The inventory is intentionally inclusive of many different types of values, but don't let that overwhelm you. Just look at the words and put a mark next to any that particularly resonate with you.

Since values typically seem virtuous, it can be hard to choose. However, it is less helpful to identify a long laundry list of values. Prioritize those that are most important to you. Once you've noted ten ideal values, narrow that list down by putting a star next to the top two to six. When I conduct this exercise in my workshops, it takes people typically less than fifteen minutes to identify their ideal values.

Search for Your Shadow Values

My experience with countless executives and students is that becoming aware of their shadow values is not particularly difficult to do. Most of us intuitively know what our shadow values are, even if we hesitate to admit them.

Think of what you value but are not comfortable *saying* you value.

If you're stumped, take a moment to think about a time when you may have felt wrongly accused. If you haven't been owning a shadow value, it is still there; it's just stuffed deep down inside. However, our shadow values tend to come out in our words or actions in ways we don't intend. Other people are likely to respond to our behavior in ways we might not expect or appreciate, even accusing us of something we hadn't realized we'd done.

For example, I felt accused by my mom of being too self-involved to answer the phone. Though she never came right out and said it, her comments led me to feel it, as when she'd say, "But you have time to call your friends!" I asked myself what values I might hold that could lead me to feel accused by my mom in this way. I had to admit that I have an autonomous streak that led me to create the boundaries that sometimes annoyed my mother. Bingo! Autonomy: I cared about freedom to use my time the way I wanted, but I wasn't comfortable admitting it because I'd been taught to prioritize others' needs and preferences.

If you're still finding it hard to admit that you care about a shadow value, it can help to remember that somewhere, someone else likely holds it as an ideal value, due to messages he or she received that were different from yours.

In my workshops, people tend to identify one or two of their own shadow values easily. Put a check mark next to the one to two that seem most relevant to the situation you're thinking about.

Tensions Within Ourselves and What to Do About Them

Noticing the tensions between our own values is key to freeing ourselves from conflict with other people. Those inner tensions often prevent us from being clear about what we want in any given situation, which makes it impossible to be clear with others. When we don't know what we want, how can anyone else give it to us?

Understanding our own values gives us the clarity we need to make straightforward commitments to, and requests of, others so we can move forward in a productive way.

Tensions Between Your Shadow and Ideal Values

Bob was incensed about Sally's refusal to accept a pay cut. He felt she cared about her own interests over the company's performance, so much so that she was willing to ruin their friendship and put him into a very difficult situation with their VC investors.

His lack of goodwill and trust turned into the silent treatment. The two had barely talked to each other for weeks, which was costly to the company because it prevented them from moving ahead efficiently on client projects, in addition to being costly to their personal relationship and extremely awkward in their small workplace. Other colleagues were stressed by their behavior and by the resulting lack of productive management.

It had gotten to the point where Bob thought that firing Sally might be his only alternative.

I asked Bob to slow down and focus on himself for a minute. What values of his own were influencing his experience with Sally?

Bob reflected on his background "growing up" in the software development field. He realized that the field prized collaboration highly. It had been drilled into him over the years that if he wanted to succeed in the software space, he'd need to be seen as a collaborative leader. Despite his natural tendency to be opinionated and his strong desire to provide direction for others, he had heeded the cultural message that it wasn't "cool" to be authoritative. He prized the ideal value of collaboration and had pushed his value of authority into the shadow. As the CEO, however, being unwilling to own his authority meant that whenever someone did something that he felt disrespected his authority—in this case, Sally's unwillingness to discuss her compensation package—his need for authority oozed out anyway, usually in an unhelpful way, such as making unreasonable demands and yelling at Sally.

Bob also noticed that another shadow value was contributing to his conflict with Sally: financial stability, for both himself and the company, was emerging as a priority for him. But that desire for stability clashed with his ideal value of risk taking. A little voice inside his head kept saying "You're an entrepreneurial risk taker just like your father and brother. Financial stability should not be your concern." Because he'd pushed his concern for stability aside, he was unaware that it was contributing to his irritation with Sally. Instead, he perceived *her* as greedy and as putting him and the company in a precarious financial position.

In fact, as Bob did, we may notice the same values in others that we reject in ourselves. In other words, we *project* our shadow values onto other people. *Projection* is a psychological process in which we defend ourselves against our shadow parts by denying those parts of ourselves and attributing them to other people instead. We distance ourselves from our shadow parts since we are not proud of them, and projecting our shadow values onto other people allows us to maintain a positive view of ourselves.

Bob's calling Sally greedy was one way for him to distance himself from the fact that he had been acting the same way she had. He had felt uncomfortable about seeking financial stability, so he pushed it into the shadow *and* he projected it onto Sally.

What can we do about this?

Own Your Projections

Have you been projecting your own shadow values onto anyone else in an unconscious effort to distance yourself from the values that you're not proud of?

Though it certainly wasn't easy, Bob was able to admit that he might have been projecting onto Sally by calling her greedy. He was able to see that doing so had been an attempt to relieve himself of his fear that his own desire for financial stability was not okay.

Notice the Tensions

Shadow values and ideal values are two sides of the same coin. We hold an ideal value in public while we inwardly hold a shadow value that is inherently in tension with that ideal value. At some point in our development, we typically learned that in order to hold our ideal value, we couldn't also hold our shadow value. But in reality, the ideal value and the shadow value have remained in steady tension with each other, often for a very long time.

Before you can do anything about the tension, it helps to simply notice its presence.

In Bob's case, he realized that his shadow value of authority was in tension with his ideal value of collaboration and his shadow value of financial stability was in tension with his ideal value of entrepreneurial risk taking.

Search for the Both/And

We often think values are mutually exclusive, when it actually makes perfectly good sense to hold both. In my consulting practice, I call this idea the *both/and principle*. How might your shadow and ideal values exist simultaneously? I discussed the both/and principle with Bob, and he acknowledged that he didn't need to see being a risk taker and caring about financial stability as contradictory. He also acknowledged that he didn't have to completely deny his need for authority in order to be a collaborative leader; in fact, he saw that part of being an effective, collaborative leader included being clear about his own boundaries and needs, as well as those of others. Bob came to see that he already valued *both* entrepreneurship *and* financial stability; *both* collaboration *and* authority.

Honor Your Shadow Values

Honoring a shadow value means to think, speak, or take action in a way that acknowledges its presence. Doing this helps bring the value into conscious awareness, where it can be properly addressed. I asked Bob to tell me one thing he would do to honor each of his shadow values. He agreed to honor his shadow value of authority by asking Sally for what he needed, which was to be treated with respect and not to be yelled at. And he would honor his shadow value of financial stability by sharing with Sally the company's financial overview and letting her know which aspects of it (in addition to her compensation) concerned him and how he thought the company could regain its financial footing.

Tensions Among Your Ideals

It can be equally difficult to deal with conflicts caused by tensions within your own set of ideal values. This happens when two or more values that you're proud of seem to be in conflict with one another.

Consider the turmoil my student Maya was in. Every year around the December holidays, Maya fought with her husband. They were both devout Hindus, but he had grown up in a family that enjoyed celebrating Christmas. Maya was uncomfortable with that, since to her mind, it was not appropriate for Hindus to celebrate holidays that weren't their own. She would have been fine if her husband's family had been Christian and invited her to celebrate Christmas with them, but they weren't! Maya faced a choice each holiday season: attend the Christmas brunch, seething with resentment, or refuse to attend the gathering and offend the family. Either way, her actions created upheaval and put her husband into the awkward position of trying to keep the peace between her and his parents.

What to do?

Notice Your Internal Tensions

It helps to recognize the tension inside yourself. When Maya identified her ideal values, she realized that her value of authenticity had eclipsed one of her other values, which was love. She wanted to be loving toward all people, not only toward people who did things her way. With that insight, she could admit that by refusing to attend the Christmas brunch, she hadn't been very loving toward her husband's family. She was able to recognize that her own seemingly conflicting ideal values contributed to the conflict between herself, her husband, and her in-laws.

Search for the Both/And

Maya asked herself how she might remain authentic to her roots while also expressing love for her husband and his family. She wondered if perhaps they could celebrate their Hindu heritage while spending time together on a holiday that was important to her husband's family.

Close Your Value/Behavior Gap

Your behavior may not always be in alignment with your values. It can be hard to admit this. Maya cringed upon realizing that although love was one of her ideal values, she hadn't been acting very lovingly toward her husband's family. Once she saw the gap between her value of love and her less-than-loving behavior, she knew she had to bring them into alignment.

She closed the gap by doing something loving: attending the Christmas brunch. And to fulfill her commitment to authenticity, she and her husband brought traditional Hindu delicacies to the brunch. The family concluded their meal by taking a photo in front of a Christmas tree topped with a statue of the Hindu goddess of love.

How Our Values Clash with Others' Values and What to Do About It

Even when we have acknowledged our own ideal and shadow values, the differences between our values and other people's can be quite challenging to deal with. By heightening our awareness of these differences, we can learn to break the conflict pattern.

When Ideal Values Clash

The most obvious way that values conflict is when our ideal values oppose others' ideal values. We see these clashes most strikingly in long-standing polarized issues such as abortion, gun control, the death penalty, and gay marriage. Clashes of ideal values can be especially intense when we feel a moral obligation to win the case.

But ideal values don't clash only in the realm of social issues. Clashes of ideal values can be especially stark when they arise as a result of differences in identity characteristics such as age, gender, race, nationality, or religion. For instance, when people of different generations hold different values, behavior that seems right to a person of one generation may seem wrong to someone from another.

Take the now-classic case of millennials and baby boomers in the workplace. As millennials have risen up the ranks and begun to outnumber their elder colleagues at work, the power dynamics that once dictated whose values took precedence have shifted. I once met two executives at a large, influential start-up who were locked in a polarizing argument about their work process. The leader of their division had called me in to try to help them work it out.

One of the executives was twenty-nine years old; the other, fifty-five. The elder executive felt the younger was moving too quickly and missing key steps in their business process. The younger one felt the elder was too slow and would cause their projects to fail if she always needed to dot every *i* and cross every *t*. I sensed that their conflict represented an intergenerational clash that was also playing out in other ways across the company which had manifested in a particularly acute way between them. I told the head of the division that if he wanted to address the issue successfully, it would be smart to engage senior leaders at the company in a conversation about it. Instead, I soon learned that the thirty-year-old CEO of the company, to whom the head of the division reported, had made a swift decision to fire the elder executive. I later learned that others at the company had interpreted that as a vote of confidence in the younger executive's perspective: speed was of paramount value at the company, even when it came at the expense of clarity and business protocol.

Given differences in ideal values based on a myriad of characteristics, including age, how can we best handle these knotty dilemmas?

Honor Others' Values

Honoring other people's values means to think, speak, or take action in a way that acknowledges their values and their right to hold them (even though you may not like or agree with those values).

One practical reason to do this is that doing the opposite—trying to convince others that their values are wrong—tends not to work. Pioneering psychological research on self-affirmation led by the social psychologist Dr. Claude Steele suggests that it is nearly impossible to change someone else's point of view, especially on an issue tied to their values, and that people generally become more adamant about their views when their values are directly challenged. Rather than try to change their values, try to accept that they have just as much right to hold theirs as you do yours.

Search for the Both/And

What if the CEO in the start-up with the two quarreling executives had tried to find a way to honor both the value of speed and the value of a clear business process without ruling in favor of one or the other? Though speed might have been seen as a greater competitive advantage, a clear process was probably not far behind in importance. Challenge yourself to find ways to honor both values, especially when it seems easier to choose only one.

Notice the Overlaps

Look for overlaps between your own and others' values that you haven't been appreciating. I conduct an exercise in my course in which I ask students to argue both sides of a divisive social issue. When they do, they often notice similar underlying values driving each position. This can be surprising for students because, like most of us, they assume that when they disagree with someone, especially about a polarized social or moral issue, it means they do not share core values with that person.

Take Mary and her Uncle Joe, who had the same bitter debate every time they saw each other. Mary argued that US borders should remain open to international refugees needing escape from persecution and economic hardship. Uncle Joe insisted that open borders leave the country vulnerable to security risks and should be tightened instead.

When I asked her to identify the ideal values guiding her argument, Mary said social justice, as well as freedom and empathy for the downtrodden. When I asked her to identify her uncle's values, she guessed that he was driven by concerns about safety and freedom for US citizens and love of country. This helped her see that although they expressed their values in different ways and were concerned about different groups of people, she and her Uncle Joe both valued freedom and care for others. Though they differed in some fundamental ways, they had more in common than either of them had been willing to admit. When Mary pointed out the overlaps to Uncle Joe, they gained a new sense of mutual understanding, which made their future conversations more tolerable than they had been in the past.

Acknowledging that we share values with people with whom we fundamentally disagree can be unsettling at first, but it can also create a much deeper sense of empathy for them. It helps us see that we and they are not as different as we initially thought.

Conflicts Due to Others' Shadow Values

Other people's shadow values are hard to perceive and all too easy to misinterpret. They themselves may not understand or acknowledge their values, so it's no wonder.

What can you do when this happens?

Own Your Projections and Attributions

You may not know, or may have misread, what someone's shadow values are. There are two psychological biases that can lead us down a dangerous path when it comes to assessing other people's shadow values. The first is *projection*, which we discussed earlier. Our tendency to project our own shadow parts onto other people can mean that in an effort to feel better about ourselves, we push the parts of ourselves that we don't like onto other people. This can be hazardous to our relationships with others, since doing so may cause us . . . not to like them! Also, they will likely resist any unfair projections, especially if we make them overtly.

The *fundamental attribution error* contributes to this; it means that we attribute other people's actions to their own personality flaws, while we attribute our own actions to situational circumstances. This allows us to maintain a healthy psychological view of ourselves, but it also causes us to think more poorly of others than perhaps we should.

If our thinking is laced with biases, why, you might ask, should we try to assess other people's values at all?

Regardless of how much (or little) you know about other people's backgrounds, you will likely notice factors that have influenced their worldview, even if they themselves are loath to admit them. The things you notice may help explain why they are behaving the way they are, which even they may not fully understand, appreciate, or acknowledge.

This can enable you to develop greater empathy for them, which is likely to have a freeing effect on *you*. As the poet Henry Wadsworth Longfellow wrote, "If we could read the secret history of our enemies, we should find in each man's life sorrow and suffering enough to disarm all hostility." Thinking about others' history will help you break free from the conflict loop.

Simply put, even if you are wrong about other people's shadow values, the rewards of thinking about them are worth the risks.

Identify Others' Shadow Values

It can be helpful to consider what others might care about but that they are unwilling to admit they care about. One way to do this is to notice what exactly they have done that troubles you and then ask yourself what about their background might lead them to act that way.

When I asked Bob what most triggered him about Sally's behavior, he told me that it was her greediness. I encouraged him to see if he could find an explanation for her behavior, and I asked him to put himself into her shoes: "Given what you know about Sally and her background—thinking both about her current life situation and whatever you may know about her family and her upbringing—what do you think might lead her to act the way she does?" Bob paused, thinking deeply about the question. He remembered a frigid winter trip to the Midwest, when Sally had a made a comment about her family losing heat more than once as a child when the bills hadn't been paid. He realized that having grown up in a poor family, she was probably concerned about financial security. "She's afraid," he said. "She's worried she won't have what she needs." He still saw her concern as exaggerated, but he was willing to concede that fears about her financial security could well account for her stubbornness and the way she had lashed out at him.

Honor Others' Shadow Values

Those insights paved the way for Bob to begin a productive dialogue with Sally. The next time they spoke, he decided, he wouldn't push a predetermined package on her. Instead, he'd start by telling her that he was committed to creating a package that would take her long-term needs into account. As he imagined the conversation, he realized right away that it would mean a lot to Sally, even if it was difficult for her to talk about her financial concerns directly. With this new plan, he was excited to give the conversation another try— a shift that was itself a major breakthrough in the psychological logjam of the past months.

Your Turn

Identify Others' Ideal and Shadow Values

To help you continue to make breaks in the conflict pattern in your situation, just as you identified your own ideal and shadow values earlier in this chapter, take a moment to try to identify others' values now. This exercise offers a powerful way to develop empathy for others by suggesting possibilities about their perspectives and behavior that you haven't yet considered.

Of course, you can't know for certain what other people's values are unless you ask them. And because they may not be consciously aware of all of their values, even if you do ask, they may be unable to talk about some of them. Also, as I noted earlier, projection and the fundamental attribution error can cause you to incorrectly identify other people's values. That said, in my experience with hundreds of clients and students, I've found that the potential rewards of trying to identify others' values are worth the risk, especially if you take measures to lower the risk by following the instructions.

First, reflect on anything you know about how they grew up, including influences from their parents, extended family members, teachers, friends, and coaches, as well as the cultural experiences they may have had at school, at work, and in the communities of which they are or once were a part. What messages were they likely to receive from those people or in those places that might influence their behavior today? Write your answers down.

Now go back through the Values Inventory and select two to three values you think might be ideal for them and write those down.

Next, try to identify their shadow values. When a value is in the shadow, the person who holds that value is likely to vacillate between two extreme ends of behavior with respect to the shadow value, as was the case with me in the situation with my mom. Whenever my mom called, either I wouldn't answer the phone and I'd feel guilty, or I'd talk until whenever *she* was ready to end the call and feel resentful. Because my value of autonomy was in the shadow, I had no way of clearly articulating it, never mind honoring it. Instead, it came out in those two extreme, unhelpful ways.

If it is hard for you to identify their shadow values, you can note your experience of their behavior and write a shadow value that might be behind it. Remember, one person's shadow value may be another person's ideal value. It all depends on the messages we received and the ways we interpreted those messages when we were growing up. The values on the right-hand side of the table that follows are examples of values that might underlie the behavior that you are attributing to them on the left-hand side of the table (shown in pairs of extremes).

YOUR INTERPRETATION OF THEIR BEHAVIOR	THEIR POSSIBLE SHADOW VALUES
Greedy *or* overly generous	Financial security
Passive-aggressive *or* aloof	Competition
Excessively authoritative *or* weak	Authority
Overly controlling *or* distant	Love
Power-hungry *or* aloof	Leadership
Status-seeking *or* detached	Recognition
Overly driven *or* lazy	Achievement

TABLE 1: The shadow values that may underlie others' behavior.

Create a Values Map

Using the lists of ideal and shadow values you've already created, write down your own ideal and shadow values in two columns and, underneath that, those of one other person (or one other group) in the situation you identified at the end of the introduction. If you'd like to include values for multiple people or groups, you can find Values Map templates accommodating various different configurations of people at optimaloutcomesbook.com/valuesmaps

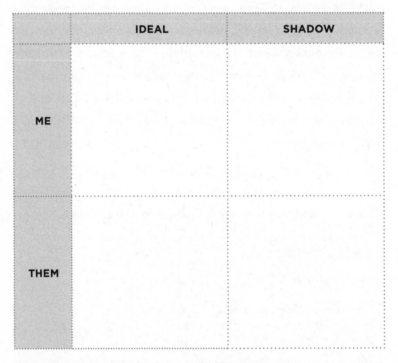

	IDEAL	SHADOW
ME		
THEM		

TABLE 2: A Values Map to help you identify values that overlap or clash inside yourself and between you and other people.

Now consider any values overlaps. Are the values you listed in any of the boxes the same as or similar to one another? If so, circle them and draw lines between them.

Next, look for values that clash and draw lines between them with arrows pointing away from each other to denote the tension between them. Many clients draw thicker, darker arrows to represent major tensions and smaller, thinner ones for clashes with less tension.

Look for overlaps and tensions among all four boxes; in other words, among your own ideal and shadow values and between your own values and others' values.

What do you notice? Are there tensions between your ideal and shadow values or between your own ideal values? Are there tensions between your own values and others' values, either ideal or shadow? Are there any overlaps between your own and others' values? If so, which ones?

Do any of the tensions or overlaps you've noticed surprise you? If so, how?

Honor Your Shadow Values

Once you've noticed the tensions between your own ideal and shadow values, choose to honor one shadow value of yours that seems most relevant to your situation. First, seek to understand why it became a shadow value for you. Was it implicitly impressed upon you, so you haven't been fully aware of it? What messages did you receive at some point in life that might have led you to suppress it? You don't have to spend lots of time on this. In fact, thinking too much might lead you down the wrong path. Simply settle yourself into a quiet space, read the following questions, and write down whatever first comes to mind.

* How or when did I first develop this value?

* How or when did I first learn this value was *not* okay?

* Which of my ideal values might this shadow value be in tension with? Considering the both/and principle, how does my shadow value coexist with that ideal value? Write down at least three ways you currently express each value in thoughts, words, or actions.

* Can I acknowledge that one value does not negate the other? That I already express both simultaneously in my life?

* How will I honor my shadow value by thinking about, talking about, or acting on it constructively? What words or actions, if any, will I say or do?

When I answered these questions, I realized that I love the autonomy that comes from being alone. I have many good memories of being alone as a child, sitting on a tiny rocking chair at a kid-sized "desk"—a shelf that my dad had mounted on the wall in the bedroom I shared with my brother—surrounded by tin cans filled with half-used crayons, semi—dried out markers, and watercolors, and reams of old paper that my grandfather brought us from the factory he worked in. I'd sit for hours, doodling, drawing, and painting pictures. My parents encouraged this. They seemed to enjoy the artwork I produced, and I enjoyed the time alone to spend as I wanted.

When did I learn that autonomy was not okay? Maybe it was when I entered kindergarten and I was expected to ride the bus to school and be part of a classroom community. And the cultural messages I got as I grew older—be nice, help others, take care of their feelings—surely pushed my value of autonomy into the shadow, if it wasn't there already.

When I looked at my ideal and shadow values side by side, I saw that my shadow value of autonomy seemed to be in tension with my ideal value of love. In the past, it had seemed to my mother, and to me as well, that I could not *both* protect my time *and* express love for her. But nothing could be further from the truth. I knew I could honor my need for autonomy—which had been the foundation of feeling like a contributing member of a loving family as a young child—and also show my love for my mother.

I asked myself how I already did this on a regular basis. Well, I worked hard *and* I spent time with my parents on the weekends. I went on solo retreats *and* I told my mom that I loved her. I took walks alone every day, *and*, despite her protestations, I did call her on occasion. I expressed autonomy *and* love in my life, even if I hadn't previously admitted how important my boundaries were to me.

I decided that day, in front of my class, that I could *both* be loving toward my mom *and* set appropriate boundaries around my time. I identified specific times of the day when I would call her and times that I would let her know were, and weren't, good to call me.

Honor Others' Shadow Values

It's time to honor a shadow value of someone else on your map. Which of his or her shadow values will you honor?

Consider why this value might be in the shadow for that person. You may have no way of knowing exactly how or when he or she first developed it, but even just thinking about it can raise your empathy for that person, so it's still a useful exercise. And when you do know the other person well, you may be surprised at how easy it is for you to answer the following questions plausibly:

* What circumstances or messages might have led the person to originally develop this value?

* What circumstances or messages might he or she have received suggesting that it was *not* okay to hold?

Thinking about my mother's values produced a giant "Aha!" For my mother, I suspected that *love* and *family closeness* were ideal values, but I also had a hunch that certain ways of expressing love might be in the shadow. "Call me more often" was her way of saying "I love you, and I'm afraid you don't love me."

When I thought about the context in which my mom had grown up, which I had learned about from stories she'd told me over the years, I noticed that it had some striking similarities to *The Marvelous Mrs. Maisel*'s New York of the 1950s, where love was present but not always clearly articulated. When my mom was growing up, teasing or even criticizing others might have been considered a form of expressing love.

Realizing that we both shared love as a value but might have had different ways of expressing it helped me feel common cause with my mother again. I was able to see that her criticism, as painful as it was, was coming from a place of love. Surely we could work through this.

Finally, list constructive ways you can acknowledge the other person's shadow value through thoughts, words, or actions (even if you do them only privately).

I wanted to find a tangible way to remember that my mom loves me. I benefited from a clever assist provided by one of my teaching assistants, Kailen, which I never would have thought of myself. Kailen took my cell phone, and in place of my mother's photo in my address book (which had been blank), she created a circle with the words "Mom Loves You" inside it. Several years later it still pops up on my phone whenever my mom calls, and it provides me with exactly the reminder I need: the only reason my mom is ever calling me is that she loves me.

Close the Gap Between Your Ideal Values and Actions

Looking back at your list of ideal values, think about how well your behavior reflects each of your ideal values. Can you identify a gap between any of your ideal values and your behavior in the situation you've been facing? For any gaps between an ideal value and your behavior, write down what actions you will take to close the gap.

When I did this exercise, I was embarrassed to notice a large gap between my ideal value of love and my own behavior. I *said* that love was a priority, but I was refusing to call or answer the phone when my own mother called! How loving was that? Not very. (I also noticed that I had been projecting onto my mother: I was accusing her of not being loving toward me, when I was guilty of the exact same behavior.)

I identified actions I could take to close the gap between my ideal value of love and my behavior: I'd do my best to pick up the phone when she called, but if I couldn't, I'd text back to suggest a time that worked for me. And I'd call my mom more regularly (I chose Wednesday mornings before work and Sunday mornings along with my kids).

Choosing Whether and How to Discuss Values

You may want to talk with the other person or people in your situation about the insights you've taken away from these exercises. That may be well advised, but before moving full steam ahead, take a moment to consider whether—and how—to have that discussion.

You can read the following guidelines now, but after you develop your Pattern-Breaking Path in Practice 6, if you've decided at that point to discuss values, I recommend that you return to review them.

Test for Readiness

Values can be tricky to talk about, especially when they seem to clash. You could be walking into a minefield. Ask yourself the following questions:

Is It Necessary?

My experience helping hundreds of executives and students use this methodology is that, much of the time, it is *not* necessary to discuss values explicitly with others in order to free yourself from conflict. What *is* necessary is for you to free yourself from the situation by changing the way you view it. Using the previous exercises to honor your own and others' values can achieve this without any involvement on the part of other people. If you think your own change in behavior toward others will be enough to turn the situation around, you may not need to discuss values with them. However, if you think that your behavior changes may make others wonder what's up and it will be helpful to let them know why you're making changes and ask for cooperation, or if your relationship is close enough that you sense that a conversation with them would be helpful, continue to the following two questions.

Am I Ready to Say It Kindly?

Going into a conversation about values when you're feeling resentful or angry creates a high risk of escalating tensions. If you feel confident that you've developed the capacity to speak kindly, great; move on to the next question. If not, practice in a role-play with a friend or coach. Once you can stay in an empathetic frame of mind for more than a few minutes, ask yourself: Am I saying this kindly? If yes, your risk of escalating the conflict is low. There's one last question to consider, though.

Is the Other Person Ready to Talk?

What indications do you have about the other person's readiness to engage in a conversation with you on this topic? If you've asked to talk about it and they have agreed, they are probably up for it. If not, I caution you against moving ahead with a conversation *at this point*. If you sense that they are not ready, check back in a few days or weeks and wait until you get a clear signal to go ahead. Either way, at some point, you may need to request a conversation, and I'll discuss how to approach that in part III.

Caveat: If in Practice 1 you learned that you tend to shut down in the face of conflict, I certainly don't want you to use the test for readiness as an excuse to let yourself off the hook! In order to free yourself from conflict, you will need first and foremost to stop indulging in your primary conflict habit. Experiment with pushing yourself outside your comfort zone, and use the scaffolding described in the next section as a way to lower your risk rather than avoiding the conversation altogether.

Build a Scaffolding

In New York City, where I work, it's very common to see scaffolding and a shed around a building to help workers repair the structure and protect pedestrians from being hit with debris. In a conflict situation, your metaphorical scaffolding helps you to repair your relationship and emerge unscathed.

First, invite the other person to the conversation with advance notice, so they can do their own emotional preparation. Suggest a day and time for the conversation that you suspect will work well for them or, better yet, invite them to propose the date and time. The setting is also important; it should be refreshing and conducive to having a thoughtful conversation. It can signify an intentional "change of channels." If you normally fight with your spouse in your bedroom late on weeknights after the kids go to bed, suggest a conversation on a weekend during the day, on a walk outside in nature. Or if you usually have tense conversations around the boardroom table, invite colleagues out for lunch, coffee, or even a walk around the block.

Next, consider how you will maintain a constructive, empathetic presence during the conversation. For example, think through how you will remain composed should the other person become stressed or angry. Would it help to take a short pause before each time you speak? Do you need to bring notes with you, to remind you of what you want to say and how you want to say it?

Prepare the Content

Finally, prepare the content of your conversation. Remind yourself of any overlaps between your own and others' values. Starting the conversation by highlighting what you think you have in common can be powerful. If it seems appropriate, let the other person know you appreciate that they may really care about *X* (whatever you have identified as their ideal or shadow values). Even if you are naming that shadow value for the first time, as long as you are honoring it, rather than using accusatory language, it will likely be helpful. For example, when Bob told Sally he would be sure to take her long-term financial needs into account, even though it was not something she was accustomed to discussing, he said it in such a respectful way that she was able to acknowledge it.

Also, let others know about any of your own values that seem appropriate to share. You can make a request for them to acknowledge your values, even if they don't agree with them. But remember, your goal is to free yourself from conflict, not to convince them that you're right.

At some point in the conversation, you should feel a sense of "breaking out" of the conflict pattern. It might even feel as though the loop that had been going around and around in circles has suddenly been broken. Once this happens, allow the conversation to wind down. Going forward, this conversation can be a reminder of your best intentions.

Chapter Summary

* Unlike *ideal values*, which we're proud to hold openly, *shadow values* are hard for us to admit, even to ourselves. Because we're in denial about them, we're often unaware that they lead us to speak and act in ways that keep us stuck in the conflict loop.

* Ideal values and shadow values differ widely from person to person. This is because messages about what is okay and

not okay to value are different from home to home, community to community, and organization to organization.

* Values can conflict in multiple ways. The most obvious way is when your own ideal values seem to clash with others'. But your ideal values can also conflict with one another inside yourself. And your shadow values can seem to clash with your ideal values, driving your behavior without your conscious awareness and causing misunderstandings with others. This is also true when it comes to other people's shadow values. Because they're unable to admit to them, dealing with them head-on can be tricky.

* Simply seeking to identify and acknowledge the existence of your own and others' ideal and shadow values—even when you don't like or agree with those values—can help break the conflict pattern.

* Considering others' shadow values can enable you to develop greater empathy for them, which is likely to have a freeing effect on *you*. Thinking about others' history will help *you* break free from the conflict loop.

Apply the Practice

HONOR IDEAL AND SHADOW VALUES

Keeping in mind the conflict situation that you wrote down at the end of the introduction:

✳ *Identify your ideal values.* Using the Values Inventory in appendix 1, identify your own ideal values—the ones that you are proud to hold openly.

✳ *Identify your shadow values.* Using the Values Inventory in appendix 1, identify your own shadow values—the ones that you are not proud of.

✳ *Estimate others' values.* Using the Values Inventory in appendix 1, see if you can identify some of the ideal and shadow values of one other person or group on your conflict map. You can't know what they are for sure, but take your best guess. Doing so will help increase your empathy.

✳ *Map the values.* Using the Values Map on page 106, write out all the values you've identified, and note any overlaps (similarities) and tensions (differences) between values. Use circles, lines, and colors to show the overlaps and tensions between and among your own and others' values.

✳ *Honor your shadow value.* Choose one of your shadow values that seems most relevant to your situation. Notice which of your ideal values it might be in tension with. Considering the both/and principle, how does your shadow value already coexist with that ideal value? Write down at least three ways in which you currently express each value in thoughts, words, or actions. How will you honor your shadow value by thinking about, talking about, or acting on it constructively? Write these down as a reminder of your commitment.

✴ *Own your projections.* Is it possible that you've been project-ing your shadow values onto others? If so, can you honor those values for yourself now?

✴ *Close the gap between your ideal values and your behavior.* Think about how well your behavior in your situation has reflected each of your ideal values. Is there a gap between any of your ideal values and your behavior in the situation you've been facing? For any gaps between an ideal value and your behavior, write what actions you will take to close the gap.

✴ *Honor their shadow value.* Choose one of the other per-son's shadow values that seems relevant to your situa-tion. What might have led them to originally develop that value? What circumstances or messages might they have received suggesting that value was *not* okay to hold? How can you acknowledge their shadow value through con-structive thoughts, words, or actions (even if you do so only privately)?

You can download a Values Practice Packet that will walk you through the work of this chapter, including a printable version of the Values Inventory and Values Maps for multiple people at:
optimaloutcomesbook.com/values

How to Achieve an Optimal Outcome

PART I	UNDERSTANDING THE CONFLICT LOOP
Practice 1	Notice Your Conflict Habits and Patterns
PART II	BREAKING THE CONFLICT PATTERN
Practice 2	Increase Clarity and Complexity: Map Out the Conflict
Practice 3	Put Your Emotions to Work for You
Practice 4	Honor Ideal and Shadow Values—Yours and Theirs
PART III	FREEING YOURSELF FROM THE LOOP

Freeing Yourself
from the Loop

✳

Imagine Your Ideal Future

Even if it were ever possible to know the answer to the question, "Who started this fight?" it would not solve the problem of needing to know, "What should we do now?"

—SYLVIA BOORSTEIN

Welcome to the section you've been waiting for. It's finally time to learn how to exit the conflict loop.

Parts I and II helped you pause to understand a conflict situation and break the conflict pattern of the past. However, there's so much self-reinforcement in any conflict loop that simply breaking the pattern doesn't enable you to leave the loop. It's easy to get sucked back in. Though you've done well by breaking the pattern, you still need something else to exit the loop.

There are two forces that will help you do this. You can be pushed out of the loop from the inside, or you can be pulled out of the loop from the outside.

In the case of a well-worn conflict loop, you'll need to do both.

The force from the outside that you'll need to pull you out of the conflict loop is your Optimal Outcome. But since we haven't yet determined exactly what your Optimal Outcome is (we'll do that in Practice 8), we'll need to start with something simpler: a prototype of it. A prototype is a concept that comes from design thinking. It refers to a preliminary model from which later forms are developed.

We'll call the prototype of your Optimal Outcome your Ideal Future; it is the "beta version" of what will become your Optimal Outcome. In Practice 8, you will have the opportunity to refine your prototype until it represents the best thing you can imagine happening, while taking into account the reality of the situation and the people you're working with.

For now, your Ideal Future will pull you in the direction you imagine, just as the magnetic pull that comes from the North Pole pulls the needle of a compass toward it.

As we discussed in the introduction, one of the reasons that some conflict situations resist resolution is that we are so focused on what happened in the past and on who is to blame (whether ourselves or others, as we saw in Practice 1) that we don't consider what we would like to happen in the future. And even if we do, our hopes tend to be vague and focused on what we want to stop happening (rather than on what we want to happen), such as when we exasperatedly call out in the heat of conflict, "This has got to stop!" Or "I just can't take it anymore!" To put it mildly, these are not clearly laid-out visions of the future we hope to create.

Even if we do know what we want and we're able to brainstorm ways to achieve it, in a recurring conflict situation, the options we come up with tend not to solve the problem. In a situation that has resisted resolution, nine times out of ten, we're not stuck because of a lack of ideas, even very good ones. On the contrary, most likely we've already tried and exhausted a long list of potentially good solutions.

We're stuck for reasons that go beyond rational thinking and problem solving. In fact, complex problems involving challenging emotions and deeply held values are typically resistant to rationally derived solutions. As the Nobel Prize–winning behavioral economist Daniel Kahneman has said, "We think, each of us, that we're much more rational than we are. And we think that we make our decisions because we have good reasons to make them. Even when it's the other way around. We believe in the reasons, because we've already made the decision. . . . Emotions such as fear, affection, and hatred explain most of the occasions on which people depart from rationality." The point is, if the problem is rooted in deeply held emotions or values, rationally derived options often do not solve the problem since they do not adequately address the emotional and unconsciously driven sources of the problem.

That is why I am *not* asking you to put on your brainstorming or problem-solving hat.

I am asking you to use your imagination instead.

You need clarity about what would truly satisfy you so you can take targeted actions toward a goal and communicate to others exactly what you are aiming for so they can help you achieve it.

Don't worry too much right now about the reality of the situation you're facing. We'll make sure that your Ideal Future is feasible—in other words, that it takes the reality of your situation and the reality of other people's preferences and needs into account—in Practice 8. For now, your job is to imagine in as much detail as possible the future you desire for yourself.

Use All of Your Senses

To gain clarity about your Ideal Future, using all five of your senses and generating the emotions you would like to experience in the future, imagine what it would look, sound, taste, smell, and feel like (tactilely and emotionally) to be in that future state.

When you try to do this, you'll run up against the fact that Western culture has traditionally emphasized the importance of only two of our five senses: seeing and hearing. Our overreliance on these two senses has detracted from our ability to engage our imaginations to their fullest capacity. In his book *The Moral Imagination: The Art and Soul of Building Peace*, the intractable-conflict expert John Paul Lederach wrote, "We more intentionally value and therefore develop perception and understanding of the universe . . . through the partial use of two senses: hearing and seeing. . . . We necessarily must engage the fuller range of senses, which includes but goes beyond the world of words."

In order to engage the fuller range of your senses, close your eyes and imagine not only what you would like to see and hear in the future but also what you would like to taste, touch, and smell and what emotions you'd like to experience. Your job is to do this until it seems as if you are experiencing the future before it arrives.

"I Have a Dream"

The United States recently marked the fiftieth anniversary of the assassination of the civil rights activist Dr. Martin Luther King, Jr. He is recognized as having delivered one of the most inspiring and impactful speeches in modern history before a crowd of more than 200,000 people who gathered at the March on Washington for Jobs and Freedom on August 28, 1963, to demand civil rights for African Americans. He stood in front of the Lincoln Memorial and gave what became known as his "I Have a Dream" speech.

Have you ever thought about why this speech is so compelling? Like many Americans, you may have learned in grade school that it is because Dr. King used the power of oratorical repetition by repeating the phrase "I have a dream" to keep us engaged and interested.

But if you listen carefully, you'll notice something else King did that I believe is even more powerful: he drew upon the five senses and emotions to help us imagine the Ideal Future he wanted to create. This is a powerful practice because the imagined future registers at a different level of our awareness from the intellectual one. We see, hear, feel, touch, and taste the Ideal Future because King not only paints a picture of it but also creates a song, a feel, a touch, and even a taste to it. He uses words to help us imagine the future he would like to create. He describes not only the scenery and the sounds but also the tactile sensations, and he even whets our appetite for what we will taste when we reach his Ideal Future. By doing all this, he helps it seem as if we're already there.

For example, he says, "Now is the time to lift our nation from the quicksands of racial injustice to the solid rock of brotherhood." By describing how the ground will *feel* beneath our feet, moving from "quicksands" to "solid rock," he distinguishes between where we are now and where he wants us to be.

When he says, "I have a dream that one day on the red hills of Georgia the sons of former slaves and the sons of former slave owners will be able to sit down together at the table of brotherhood," he whets our appetite to *taste* the food at the feast of fellowship in his Ideal Future.

When he says, "I have a dream that one day even the state of Mississippi, a state sweltering with the heat of injustice, sweltering with the heat of oppression, will be transformed into an oasis of freedom and justice," he helps us *feel* the "heat of oppression" and the relief of touching the cool waters of an oasis in his Ideal Future.

He helps us *feel* the skin of the children holding hands with one another in his Ideal Future. He says, "I have a dream that one day . . . right there in Alabama, little black boys and black girls will be able to join hands with little white boys and white girls as sisters and brothers."

When he calls out, "This will be the day when all of God's children will be able to sing with a new meaning, 'My country, 'tis of thee, sweet land of liberty, of thee I sing. Land where my fathers died, land of the pilgrim's pride, from every mountainside, let freedom ring,'" King helps us *hear* the tune of the song and the chime of the bells of freedom ringing.

Imagine Your Ideal Future

Now, there is a fine line between a successful "I Have a Dream" speech about a future that inspires you and a pipe dream. The line can sometimes be tough to distinguish. But the only way to distinguish one from the other is to gain clarity about what you're shooting for in the first place.

For now, your work is simply to imagine an Ideal Future without worrying about how feasible it is. We'll come to that work soon enough.

When Bob imagined an Ideal Future, it had two parts. First, he imagined proposing a compensation package to Sally that he, the CFO, the VC investors, and Sally could all agree upon. He could sense his feeling of elation when he heard Sally say that his proposal seemed fair to her.

Second, he imagined sharing good times with Sally again. He visualized their walking into one of their favorite restaurants to treat a potential client to dinner and laughing and having a great meal. He could smell the red wine and taste the food that the chef had prepared for them. He imagined their developing a deeper sense of understanding of and trust in each other, having gotten through this tough time together. He imagined the positive impact it would have on the client they'd taken out for dinner, who would sense the warmth of their friendship and benefit from their renewed ability to collaborate with each other.

In the past several years, when I have asked students to choose a conflict to work through in my class, a large majority of them have chosen something personal. But among my early cohorts, it was less common. It made sense that my student Camilla was the outlier. She was from a giant Italian American family who all lived within a few blocks of one another in Brooklyn. She couldn't talk about her family without smiling; it became clear that her family was deeply involved in every aspect of her life. So when a conflict suddenly arose, it troubled her deeply.

At the young age of thirty-five, one of her cousins, Vincent, had passed away unexpectedly, leaving behind his wife, Tammy, and five-year-old son, Dylan. The family's relationship with Tammy had been strained throughout her seven-year marriage to Vincent, and after Vincent's traumatic loss, the strain became even more intense. Vincent's mother was lobbying for Dylan to live with her; other family members believed that Tammy was capable of taking care of Dylan on her own, but they wanted to keep a much closer eye on Dylan as he grew up.

Either way, Tammy was painfully aware that the family didn't trust her to raise her own son. And though Dylan was still a young boy, she knew he was picking up on the hostility that surrounded him. Camilla was the only person in the family in whom Tammy had confided and trusted.

Camilla felt saddened and overwhelmed by the situation. She felt caught between Tammy and the rest of the family, especially Tammy's mother-in-law, who was Camilla's beloved aunt. Yet because of her strong relationship with Tammy, Camilla realized she had a unique opportunity to influence things for the better. She took seriously my suggestion to imagine a better future for her family.

Before Camilla imagined her Ideal Future, she reviewed all she had learned in the previous practices. When she first mapped out the conflict, she started with Tammy and her mother-in-law. Very quickly she realized that the conflict was broader, including all of her extended family members, particularly each of her three aunts and her mother, who were very close to one another and talked often.

In the values practice, Camilla had realized that many of the members of her family perceived a clash in values between themselves and Tammy. They viewed themselves as upholding traditional Italian family values, and they saw Tammy as embracing modern American culture instead.

Because of Camilla's close relationship with Tammy, Camilla knew that Tammy shared the family's value of tradition, even if it didn't always look that way on the outside.

Camilla also noticed that although her family ostensibly valued love, they weren't being very loving toward Tammy, and in their attempt to help Dylan, they were causing him additional pain. She knew that her family members were grieving and, perhaps as a result, weren't acting at their best. She saw a gap between their ideal value of love and their behavior.

Informed by a clearer understanding of the past, she imagined an Ideal Future for her family. She wrote:

I imagine a future where a community of nurturing develops in the family. I hear Tammy talking with my aunt, my mother, and the rest of the mothers in the family about their common interest in raising their children with good morals, family values, and a connection to each other. As a result, more understanding among them develops.

I see Dylan and his cousins playing together while Tammy and all the mothers in the family look on with a hope that the children will continue to be close and carry on our family traditions. I smell the sweet aromas from the food wafting off the stove in the kitchen, and I feel the warmth of my aunt's and Tammy's skin as we hold hands around the dining room table to give thanks for our family.

Conceive of Your Detailed Ideal Future

In order to design a Pattern-Breaking Path to your Ideal Future in the next chapter, it will help to imagine your Ideal Future with even more specificity. This might mean, as it did for Camilla, imagining the details of an event that you would like to have happen in the future.

Camilla believed that if she wanted to influence her family dynamic, she would ultimately need to have heart-to-heart conversations with the members of her family who were the most wary of Tammy. She would need to listen to them and possibly help them talk directly and calmly with Tammy about their concerns.

But right now, that seemed like too much probing in a situation that was already laden with intensity. Instead, she imagined members of the extended family, including Tammy and Dylan, cooking together.

Since Thanksgiving was approaching and the family traditionally ate the holiday meal together, Camilla imagined all the mothers and children in the family gathering together to cook the meal. She used all five of her senses and her emotions to imagine their time together. She could smell the aromas of the soups emanating from the kitchen, and she could sense the camaraderie that would envelop all the moms and kids. She could feel the warmth of the hugs that would be interspersed with the cooking. That turned out to be just the right thing to help shift the family dynamic.

Write, Draw, or Record Your "I Have a Dream" Speech

Martin Luther King, Jr., was able to inspire the masses with his dream of the future because he took the time not only to imagine it but also to put it into words.

Once you've imagined your Ideal Future in detail, your job is to write, draw, paint, collage, or audio-, video-, or otherwise record the pictures, sounds, feelings, tastes, and smells that you imagine will exist in your Ideal Future.

As part of her class assignment, Camilla wrote a paper that described her imagined future. The process of writing it down helped her gain clarity about what she wanted to happen.

In fact, research suggests that because she took the time to record what her imagined future would be like, including what she would touch, taste, and smell and what emotions she would experience, it was more likely to occur in reality than if she had simply said, "I want everyone to love one another."

Even if her Ideal Future was not feasible, it was helpful to gain clarity about what she wanted because, ironically, only once she knew what she wanted would she be able to discover whether it was attainable or not.

What is *your* "I Have a Dream" speech?

Communicate Your Ideal Future

Once you have imagined and recorded your Ideal Future in as much vivid detail as possible, in order for it to come to fruition, you may need to communicate it to the others involved in your situation. Camilla knew that her Ideal Future would have no chance of happening if she wasn't able to let her mother, aunts, and Tammy know about her idea and seek their involvement. Similarly, Bob knew his Ideal Future wouldn't have a chance if he never asked Sally to meet.

However, just like talking about values, discussing your Ideal Future can be tricky. Here are a couple of pointers to guide your conversations about your Ideal Future with others.

* *Keep it simple.* It's often neither helpful nor necessary to give other people the entire backstory about how or why you imagined your Ideal Future. All they need to know is the "what": what you hope will happen. Martin Luther King, Jr.'s, speech was only seventeen minutes long, but its impact was enormous.

* *Consider how much to reveal.* If you think there's a chance that telling others about your Ideal Future might backfire and produce the opposite of what you're aiming for, think about how much of your Ideal Future it makes sense to

discuss. You can always start by sharing a little bit of it and communicate more later on.

Now that you've thought about *what* your goal is, the next three chapters are dedicated to the question of *how* to achieve it. If there are people you'd like to share your Ideal Future with, in the next two chapters, you'll have the opportunity to consider how to do it so it has the effect you intend.

Chapter Summary

* In recurring conflicts, people are typically focused on what happened in the past and who is to blame. It can take special effort to look ahead at what you *do* want.

* When recurring conflicts are driven by deeply held emotions and values, they are often not sufficiently addressed by rational solutions.

* To deal with this, engage your imagination. Use all five of your senses and your emotions to imagine the future you'd like to create.

* Imagine not only what you would like to see and hear in the future but also what you would like to taste, touch, and smell and what emotions you'd like to experience. Do this until it seems as if you are experiencing the future before it arrives.

* Prepare to communicate about your Ideal Future so you can engage others to help you make it a reality.

Apply the Practice

IMAGINE YOUR IDEAL FUTURE

✳ *Imagine.* Take a moment to imagine your Ideal Future in as much vivid detail as possible. Use all five of your senses—seeing, hearing, touching, tasting, and smelling—as well as your emotions to imagine the best possible future situation. Remember, right now, you don't need to concern yourself with the constraints of reality—you'll do that when you get to Practice 8. For now, simply imagine an Ideal Future based on the work you've done in the previous practices.

✳ *Record.* What is *your* version of Dr. Martin Luther King, Jr.'s, "I Have a Dream" speech? Once you've imagined your Ideal Future in detail, write, draw, collage, or audio- or video-record the pictures, sounds, feelings, tastes, and smells that you imagine will exist in your Ideal Future. This will help you remember what you're shooting for, which will make it more likely to happen in reality.

✳ *Prepare to communicate.* Would it help to share your Ideal Future with anyone else? Or might telling others ironically make it harder for your Ideal Future to come to pass? If you think it makes sense to share it, whom might you tell? What will you tell them?

You can watch Dr. King's "I Have a Dream" speech (and read the transcript) to see how he helps us imagine his Ideal Future at:

https://www.newsweek.com/mlk-jr-assassination
-anniversary-i-have-dream-speech-full-text-video-870680

You can download a worksheet to help
you imagine your own Ideal Future at:
optimaloutcomesbook.com/imagine

✳

Design a
Pattern-Breaking Path (PBP)

The most basic way to get someone's attention is this: Break a pattern.

—CHIP HEATH AND DAN HEATH

In Practice 1, we identified the conflict habits that have been interacting to form a pattern that has kept you and others stuck in a conflict loop. In Practices 2, 3, and 4, you learned ways to change your perspective and your behavior to break the conflict pattern.

But since there's so much self-reinforcing momentum on any conflict loop, making breaks in the loop isn't sufficient to exit it. You'll need a "pull" from outside and a "push" from inside the loop in order to free yourself from it.

In Practice 5, you created an Ideal Future prototype to provide you with the "pull" from outside the loop to help you exit it. In this chapter, your Pattern-Breaking Path (PBP) will provide you with the "push" from inside the loop that you'll need to leave it.

In other words, in Practice 5, you imagined *what* you'd like to happen in the future; now it's time to plan *how* you will get there—what you will actually do to turn your imagined future into reality.

What Is a Pattern-Breaking Path (PBP)?

A Pattern-Breaking Path (PBP) is a linked, yet simple, set of action steps to help you exit the conflict loop and move toward your imagined Ideal Future.

Although the name of the path correctly suggests that you'll be breaking patterns, I don't want you to be like a bull in a china shop and just start breaking patterns left and right. That would leave a wake of unintended consequences to deal with on top of the tough situation you're already facing. Instead, I want you to thoughtfully design a path to exit the conflict loop.

Successful paths have three characteristics: they involve doing something surprisingly different from what has been done before; they're simple; and each action step builds on the one that comes before it.

Former president Barack Obama demonstrated these three hallmarks of a Pattern-Breaking Path when he dealt with the following racially fraught circumstance.

In July 2009, upon returning home from a trip overseas, Dr. Henry Louis Gates, Jr., the director of Harvard's Hutchins Center for African and African American Research, discovered that his front door would not open. He entered his house through the back door and asked his driver to help him open the front door from the outside. After succeeding, the driver left and Dr. Gates returned inside his home.

A few minutes later, responding to a call from a concerned neighbor about a potential break-in, Cambridge police sergeant James Crowley arrived at Dr. Gates's house. Sergeant Crowley asked Dr. Gates to step outside, and an exchange ensued that led to Dr. Gates's handcuffing and arrest for disorderly conduct.

Immediately after the exchange took place, Dr. Gates suggested that the police had assumed he was breaking in because he is black. Sergeant Crowley maintained that he had just been doing his job and would not have arrested Dr. Gates if he hadn't acted in a disorderly way. A few days later, the charges against Gates were dropped. But by then, the arrest had already provoked race-related anxiety across the nation, with the *New York Times* reporting that thousands of news stories about race had been published since the incident.

Adding fuel to the fire, when a reporter asked President Obama about the incident at an unrelated news conference, Obama responded that the police had "acted stupidly." Although he later apologized for his choice of words, his comment had done its damage. He was seen as having taken sides. Many Americans were angry and were waiting to see what would happen next.

If I were to characterize the conflict pattern in this situation, I'd call it Blame/Blame. The public account of the exchange between Sergeant Crowley and Professor Gates suggests that they got locked in a loop of blaming one another, and once the story was made public, it only led to further Blame/Blame loops.

Do Something Surprisingly Different

Embroiled in a situation that had the potential to further inflame race relations in the United States, President Obama made a pattern-breaking move. Instead of doing something that had already been done before, such as creating a task force on racial profiling that would have duplicated existing efforts or allowing the issue to fester by doing nothing at all, he did something surprising: he invited Dr. Gates and Sergeant Crowley to have a beer with him on the White House lawn. He called it an opportunity to have a drink together and mend their relationships. It was the unexpected, even surprising, nature of his invitation that had the power to break the conflict pattern.

Do Something Simple

In addition to doing something surprisingly different, it is important to keep the actions that make up your PBP simple. The simpler your movement, the easier it will be to track your impact, and the more likely the effect will be what you intend.

Think of all the grand gestures Obama could have made. He could have invited other political leaders to the White House to discuss race relations in the United States; he could have held a press conference with hundreds of journalists in attendance peppering him with questions; he could have flown to Massachusetts to meet with the Cambridge Police Department and administrators at Harvard; he could have asked members of his cabinet to organize talks on race relations. Instead, he chose something relatively simple: inviting two men to get together over a beer.

Journalists would later call the gathering "The Beer Summit," but Obama would reiterate his intention to keep things simple. He told the *New York Times*, "I heard this has been called the beer summit. It's a clever term, but this is not a summit, guys. It's three folks having a drink at the end of the day and hopefully giving people an opportunity to listen to each other."

We'll discuss additional ways to prevent unintended consequences of your actions in the next chapter. For now, keeping your actions simple is a great way to help ensure that you will eventually break free from the conflict loop.

Build Each Action on the One Before It

Although Obama's invitation was simple, it is important to note that the path he designed didn't *begin* with beer on the White House lawn. In fact, the day began with private tours of the White House for each of the two men and their families. Only after that did the men sit at a table on the White House lawn, talking over beer and pretzels.

The path didn't begin with the White House tours, either. It began with an invitation to the men and their families, which itself probably began with Obama reflecting on the future he hoped for, discussing it with trusted advisers, and developing a set of steps to make that happen.

The path extended further into the future, as well. By the end of the day, Obama said that Gates and Crowley had told him they had made plans to get together for lunch another time soon.

After the gathering, Dr. Gates told journalists that President Obama "allowed us to begin to bridge our divide and make a larger contribution to American society. . . . I don't think anybody but Barack Obama would have thought about bringing us together. . . . the president was great—he was very wise, very sage."

Of his relationship with Sergeant Crowley, Dr. Gates joked, "We hit it off right from the beginning. When he's not arresting you, Sergeant Crowley is a really likable guy."

In summary, Obama's Pattern-Breaking Path was made up of a linked set of simple action steps that were surprisingly different from what had been done before. They started off relatively small (reflecting on the existing conflict pattern and planning; inviting two men to have a drink with him) and continued to grow until the impact was more widely felt (inviting the men and their families on a tour of the White House together; holding the meeting outdoors and allowing journalists to cover it). At that point, Crowley and Gates felt good enough about their relationship that they made their own plans to get together.

As a result of Obama's efforts, an explosive issue that could have continued to rock the nation was instead stopped in its tracks and created a new path toward healing between individuals and in the larger society as the American public learned about the effects of their meeting.

Many successful Pattern-Breaking Paths start with subtle steps and build toward an apex of activity, as the beer summit did. And like the summit, which was followed up by a promise for lunch between Dr. Gates and Sergeant Crowley, many such events are followed by smaller, less formal reinforcements. But this is not set in stone.

Though your PBP should comprise action steps that, one by one, move you and others toward the Ideal Future you've imagined, you can configure your path any way you choose. We'll discuss specific ways to configure your path later in this chapter; first, let's take a look at how my student Camilla designed hers.

Design the Steps

Recall the story from Practice 5 about Camilla, whose family was torn apart by the loss of her cousin Vincent and the family's sense that Vincent's widow, Tammy, didn't share their values. After she imagined an Ideal Future, Camilla designed several steps of her Pattern-Breaking Path. Each step would provide the groundwork for the next one.

The first step of Camilla's PBP involved her morning pause practice. She sat quietly each morning and imagined love being sent back and forth, first between herself and each member of the family and then between people in the family who hadn't been seeing eye to eye, such as Tammy and Tammy's mother-in-law. She also reminded herself of her own potential role in helping to mend the family dynamic. She took the time to imagine in detail the Ideal Future she wanted to create.

The next step along her Pattern-Breaking Path involved suggesting the idea of cooking together in one-on-one conversations with Tammy, Tammy's mother-in-law, and Camilla's own mother and two other aunts. Camilla let each of them know that she was concerned about the family and that she wanted to do something to encourage love in the family at a difficult time. She then told each of them about her idea and asked if they had any objections or other ideas to add.

Once Tammy and the four mothers were on board, Camilla let the rest of the mothers in the family know about the idea. Then she organized the day, bought the cooking supplies, and hosted the event in her mother's kitchen.

Camilla did a number of things to design the steps of her PBP for success. First, she designed each step to build upon the one that preceded it. She began by working within herself. She used her pause practice to clarify her Ideal Future before she broached the idea with anyone else in the family. She set out to involve other people only once she had spent some time building a strong foundation of love of family within herself and clarifying her Ideal Future.

Second, she met with Tammy, her own mother, and each of her aunts *individually* to discuss the idea of cooking together before announcing it to the family. That ensured that each of them could communicate concerns privately with Camilla if they didn't like the idea.

Third, she took a leadership role in communicating the idea to others in the family and hosting the event.

Finally, she had realistic expectations. She didn't expect the event to suddenly take away all the pain the family had experienced. She knew that cooking together was only one step in a longer path toward wholeness for her family.

Design the Steps Along Your Pattern-Breaking Path

Now it is time to think about how you will design the steps in your Pattern-Breaking Path. Though it can be helpful to follow the listed sequence of steps, designing your path is an idiosyncratic process that works best when you take the particular details of your situation into account and build its steps based on those. I want you to design a path that frees you from the conflict loop of your situation, taking the unique nature of the existing conflict pattern into account. I don't want you to fail to break free from the loop of your own situation because you are trying to fit yourself into a preset framework of prescribed steps.

Step One: Start with Yourself

It usually helps to start with yourself and build outward from there. As you know, this book is about how to free *yourself* from conflict. The best way to free yourself is to begin by directing your attention within.

Your actions in Step One may be so subtle that only you are aware of them. For example, you might incorporate a three-minute pause practice into your daily routine. In situations that have been particularly fraught and painful, some of my students have developed their own versions of a traditional loving-kindness meditation to help their actions spring from love. They sit quietly for a few minutes and allow themselves to feel loved by someone they feel loves them unconditionally. Then they imagine themselves sending out love to some of the people on their conflict map and then to strangers in the wider world. Finally, they return to the feeling of receiving love from someone who loves them unconditionally.

Alternatively, you may spend your pause time imagining your Ideal Future in detail until you are ready to talk about it with others. Or you might spend your pause time identifying and making commitments that, based on the work you've done so far, you believe will help free you from the conflict loop, such as taking a deep breath at least once per day whenever you feel intense emotions arise within you.

Step Two: Connect with One Person

In Step Two, consider how to involve one person from your conflict map. This may not always be the most obvious other person on your map. It might be someone on your map with whom you already have a trusting relationship or someone you suspect could be helpful to you.

On the other hand, sometimes it does make sense to go directly to the person with whom you've been in a conflict pattern. Especially if you have done the work so far to gain clarity about the values involved and you've been able to settle your emotions and use them in your favor, it might be most helpful to start directly with this person.

You might ask them out for coffee (or a beer!) to hear more about their perspective and to share your Ideal Future with them. Or you might make a phone call to apologize to someone or simply to say hello. Remember to keep your actions simple *and* pattern breaking.

Step Three: Involve a Small Group

In Step Three, think about whether or how you might involve more people from your conflict map. If appropriate to your situation, maybe you could host a meeting, video chat, or phone call in which you seek to engage with, and gather new ideas and support from, other people on your map. In this step, I've seen a client request a meeting with two of the leaders of the division with whom he and his colleagues had been at loggerheads; a student ask for a call with his father in China and his aunt in New York; and a client organize a live video chat with a colleague and a grassroots organizer in the Middle East.

Step Four: Involve Larger Groups of People

In Step Four, if appropriate, you may now be ready to bring together a larger group of people who have not been seeing eye to eye. For example, in this step, I've had a client hold a meeting between the people on his research team and the people on the sales team who have not been getting along to discuss ways to collaborate more effectively; a student create a WhatsApp group for family members in the United States and China to stay in touch and remain coordinated; and a client organize an effort to reach thousands of young people on Facebook to support Middle East peace through a grassroots visual arts program.

Steps Five and Beyond: Extend the Work

Steps Five and beyond may be made up of a series of one-on-one conversations or group experiences meant to support and extend the work you did in the previous steps.

With Bob and Sally's situation, in Step One of Bob's PBP, he committed to engaging with his anger constructively. He began a practice of stopping to take a deep breath before responding, even when his anger wasn't triggered. He thought that would help him be less likely to lash out at people when his anger did get triggered. He imagined himself getting a phone call from an angry client and, instead of slamming the phone down and immediately shooting off a nasty email to the manager responsible for the mistake, stopping, breathing in and out, thinking of a constructive response, and then taking action.

For Step Two, Bob envisioned a meeting with Sally that would focus on their working relationship, not on the content of her compensation package. He realized that their relationship and the package were two separate issues and that they could not have a productive conversation about the package until they dealt explicitly with their friendship at work.

He would begin by apologizing for catching Sally off guard and yelling at her on their way back from lunch. (Even though he felt that she should apologize to him for being the first one to yell on the street, he decided to take responsibility for his own actions, regardless of whether Sally did the same or not.)

He would honor his own shadow value of authority by requesting that Sally refrain from yelling at him going forward. Without mentioning it explicitly, he would honor Sally's shadow value of financial stability by letting her know that he could understand her unease about the financial changes and was committed to doing a better job of keeping her in the loop.

Assuming that Step Two went well, in Step Three, Bob would ask the CFO to help him develop a fair package to send to Sally. In Step Four, Bob would ask Sally for a second meeting to discuss the compensation package itself. He imagined emailing a clear proposed package to Sally in advance of the meeting so she could prepare her thoughts about it. At the meeting, he would ask for her input. He would make no promises during the meeting, but he would commit to carefully considering Sally's input and then letting her know what he and the CFO determined was possible.

That would represent a big departure from Bob's previous behavior. Though he felt nervous about whether he could pull it off, he was also excited to try something different.

Let Others Know Your Intentions

Like Camilla and Bob, you may need help from other people to make a specific event happen. Alternatively, you may simply commit to acting differently without needing anyone else's involvement. For instance, maybe you will start counting to three in your head before you answer your business partner's requests, to prevent yourself from reacting in a way you'll regret later on. In this case, you don't necessarily need to let your partner know what you're up to.

In fact, surprising other people by breaking out of your old habits without advance warning can be very effective. As we've discussed, there's something about the element of surprise that can catch people off guard in a good way—and that enables *them* to respond differently as well.

However, changing your own behavior can be difficult, and if you let others know your intentions, they can help you. They can offer support and provide you with feedback so you'll know when you're on target and when you're falling short of your aims.

In their first meeting, Bob planned to let Sally know his intentions to be more genuinely collaborative and also to maintain his own authority as CEO. He would acknowledge that he would be doing his best to practice these at the appropriate times, but he might not be perfect, and he would ask for her support as well as her forgiveness.

Chapter Summary

* Though the practices in part I help you break the conflict pattern, you still need to exit the conflict loop. Your imagined future plus your Pattern-Breaking Path (PBP) provide the pull and the push you'll need to exit it.

* A Pattern-Breaking Path (PBP) is a linked, simple, surprisingly different set of action steps designed to help you exit the conflict loop and move you toward your imagined Ideal Future.

* It is important to keep the actions that make up your PBP simple. The simpler your movement, the easier it will be to track your impact and the more likely the effects will be what you intend.

* Your PBP should comprise action steps that, one by one, will move you and others toward the Ideal Future you've imagined. Though there are a series of steps that my clients and students have found useful, you can configure your path any way you choose.

Apply the Practice

DESIGN A PATTERN-BREAKING PATH (PBP)

To design a set of action steps that will help you exit the conflict loop while keeping your actions simple and surprisingly different from what has been done in the past, ask yourself the following questions.

* *Step One:* What solo or pause practice can I begin with?

* *Step Two:* Who is the first person, if any, whom I will involve? What action can I take that will be simple and surprisingly different?

* *Step Three:* Who else, if anyone, will I involve?

* *Step Four:* Are there groups of people I can engage? If so, which groups? How can I engage with them?

* *Steps Five and beyond:* How will I build a path of linked action steps from here?

You can learn more about the Beer Summit at:
https://www.nytimes.com/2009/07/31/us/politics/31obama.html

You can download a worksheet to design your own
Pattern-Breaking Path (PBP) at: optimaloutcomesbook.com/PBP

✳

Test Your Path

What makes us wise? . . . We contemplate the future. . . . The
power of prospection is what makes us wise.

—MARTIN E. P. SELIGMAN AND JOHN TIERNEY

Prevention is the best medicine.

—MORTON DEUTSCH

The more experiments you make, the better.

—RALPH WALDO EMERSON

We typically get stuck in one of two pitfalls while on a
Pattern-Breaking Path: Either we act recklessly, failing to think about the potentially unintended consequences of our actions, or we do the opposite. Anxious about the
potential consequences of our actions, we fail to think about the

potentially dire consequences of *inaction*, and we take no action at all.

One of history's most renowned feats of international diplomacy, the Camp David Accords, illustrates the pitfall of failing to think about the consequences of inaction, and how former president Jimmy Carter helped turn that around.

When Carter was elected in 1976, he committed himself to a daunting goal: brokering peace between Israel and Egypt. The countries had been in a state of war for thirty years, since Israel's founding, over control of the Sinai Peninsula and related issues. Tens of thousands of lives had been lost in the battles between Israel and Egypt and in broader regional conflicts.

Carter worked with Egyptian president Anwar Sadat, who had made overtures toward Israeli prime minister Menachem Begin that had been unsuccessful. Then Carter took a suggestion from his wife, Rosalynn, to invite the two leaders to meet in person at Camp David, the secluded presidential retreat in Maryland, for private talks.

Sadat arrived at the talks already believing that an agreement was possible. Begin, however, questioned what could be accomplished in a few days' time. Although he accepted the invitation, he was extremely cautious about what might happen if any ground (literal or figurative) was ceded to Egypt.

Despite Begin's skepticism, the talks got off to a positive start. But eventually, after several days of intense negotiations, the peace talks broke down. Sadat and Begin stormed out of a session and were unwilling to meet face-to-face again. It seemed that the two leaders would leave more divided than they had arrived.

In a final attempt to be helpful, President Carter asked his assistant to make three copies of a photo of himself smiling with Begin and Sadat that had been taken in a hopeful moment earlier in the week. He signed the photos and addressed one to each of Prime Minister Begin's three grandchildren.

President Carter knocked on the prime minister's door as he was packing to go home and handed Begin the photos. Begin looked at one photo, then the next, and the next. He read the names of his grandchildren aloud as tears rolled down his cheeks.

Seeing the photos addressed to his grandchildren forced Begin to think about the dark future he was handing not just them but their entire generation if he failed to secure peace. He stopped packing and returned to the negotiating table.

Through the simple gesture of handing Begin the photographs, Carter had successfully helped Begin realize that the unintended consequences of inaction would be starkly worse than any possible outcome of an agreement. Begin saw that his anger and frustration in the moment mattered little compared with the pain of children who would know only war. That was the real stake at hand.

Later that day, Begin made a critical concession regarding the Israeli settlements in the Sinai, and the two leaders reached their historic agreement, the Framework for Peace in the Middle East. In 1979, the two countries signed a treaty, bringing the first formal peace in three decades.

We'll return to this story a bit later in this chapter when we discuss two exercises to help you avoid the pitfalls of unintended consequences—whether due to failing to act or acting rashly. The first exercise helps you think ahead so you can predict and prevent any unintended consequences of your own actions or inactions. The second exercise involves taking small steps in the right direction through what I call "mini-experiments" to further bolster your Pattern-Breaking Path.

These exercises will provide you with balance by helping you pause to think ahead and move without delay. Together, by testing the PBP you have designed, they will boost your confidence in your PBP and help you stay on your path over the long run so you can achieve an Optimal Outcome.

What Could Go Wrong?

In Practice 5, you reoriented your focus from the negative—what went wrong in the past—toward the positive—what you would like to happen in the future. You were, in a sense, anticipating what could go *right*.

Now it's time to shift your focus toward the future to anticipate what could go *wrong*.

In life, every action you take or don't take can create both intended and unintended effects. When you're in a challenging situation, those effects can become exaggerated.

As we've discussed, due to the fundamental attribution error, we tend to think that other people's faulty actions are due to their own personality flaws, while we attribute our own actions to the circumstances in which we happen to find ourselves. In conflict situations, our negative attributions about others often go into overdrive, leading us to assume the worst of others and causing even the most unintentional of our own actions to have outsized negative impacts on how other people view us.

To account for this, it is important to think through the potential unintended effects of your actions before they occur, so you can prevent or mitigate them. If you don't do this, no matter how carefully you've thought through your PBP, you risk making things even worse than they already are.

We've already discussed how, especially when we're in conflict, our minds tend to distill complex situations into black-and-white, us-versus-them affairs to help us fight or flee. Similarly, when we're in the heat of conflict, our focus is reduced to the here and now—without much thought given to the future. If we think about the consequences of our own behavior at all, we think about the impact of our behavior *on ourselves right now.*

For example, we typically think:

* If I walk away from this person who is screaming at me, I'll feel relieved and get some peace and quiet. (I'm thinking about the impact of my own behavior—walking away—on myself right now.)

* If I hit Send on this email, I'll feel glad it's done and I can move on to other, more important matters. (I'm thinking about the impact of my own behavior—hitting Send—on myself right now.)

* If I refuse this request, I'll be able to leave work early and get to the gym. (I'm thinking about the impact of my own behavior—refuse the request—on myself right now.)

We do not usually think about the impact of our behavior on other people, and we almost certainly do not consider the potential impact of our behavior on ourselves or on others over the long term.

To correct for these errors in our thinking, it is helpful to consider the impact of your actions not only on yourself today but also on yourself and on others down the road.

In her book *10-10-10: 10 Minutes, 10 Months, 10 Years: A Life-Transforming Idea,* Suzy Welch, a former longtime editor in chief of the *Harvard Business Review,* challenged us to think about the potential impact of our actions ten minutes from now, ten months from now, and ten years from now.

I recommend adding to this practice: think about the impact of your actions not only on yourself or even on the obvious others in your situation (for Bob, that would be Sally) but on nonobvious others as well (for Bob, they could be the CFO and the investors), both now and in the future.

As we saw, President Carter helped Prime Minister Begin think about the impact of his inability to make peace on his grandchildren—the future generation. Carter successfully redirected Begin's attention *away* from himself in the *present* moment *to* his grandchildren in the *future*. That was the shift in perspective that Begin needed to compel him to return to the negotiating table and make a historic agreement. It is also worth noting that Carter's intervention was not with words but with photographs, which may have activated Begin's imagination and certainly seems to have appealed to his emotions.

Returning to Bob and Sally, let's rewind the story to the day before they had the screaming fight on the street corner. Bob knew that Sally would not be happy when he brought up the issue of her compensation. Whenever he had brought it up in the past, she had either yelled at him or shut down the conversation.

Using this exercise to think ahead, Bob could have said to himself: If I bring up Sally's compensation package informally on the street at the end of lunch tomorrow, the impact *on me in the moment* will be: I'll be relieved to finally get it off my chest. The impact *on me in ten months from now* is that her package will be reset, and the impact *on me in ten years from now* is that I'll feel glad that the company is in good financial standing.

But what about Sally? Well, Bob might have thought, if I bring it up after lunch, Sally may be uncomfortable. I'll be bringing it up without fair warning, and she'll be taken off guard. In ten months from now, she may still be shut down and angry at me, unwilling to discuss the package at all. Ten years from now, I'm not sure she'll still be at the company.

Okay, Bob might have thought, maybe bringing it up after lunch is not the best idea. What else can I do?

It is equally helpful to ask: What could be the impact of my behavior on others who aren't directly involved? Bob could have thought: If I bring this up at the end of lunch, what might be the impact on the CFO? If my attempt is unsuccessful because it catches Sally off guard and shuts down the conversation for several more months, the CFO might not be too happy, either.

This process helps you think a few steps ahead, *before* you make a move, as a chess player does on a chessboard—to optimize your outcomes and prevent disasters.

Anticipate Unintended Consequences

No matter how positive our intent, when designing a PBP, we often miscalculate the effect of our overtures. Like theater directors, we script out scenes to bring about our Ideal Future—and then we're caught off guard when the actors go off book. The trouble is that our own (starring) role is the only one we've properly fleshed out.

To prevent this, think about how your Pattern-Breaking Path might play out in the future. As Carter helped Begin do, consider not only how your own actions (or inactions) will affect yourself today, but also how your actions (or inactions) may impact the other people you identified on your conflict map in Practice 2, now and in the future.

For example, if Bob pursues his PBP, he could anticipate some possible unintended impacts on Sally:

* When I ask Sally to meet, she may agree, but in the meeting, she might get upset and start screaming at me again.

* Sally may still be too angry to discuss the package with me.

* Even if we agree on a new compensation package now, a few months from now, Sally may be unhappy with her financial situation and decide to leave for a competing firm.

This process was helpful for my student Maura, who was concerned about her brother Mike's alcohol consumption. When she tried to talk to him about it, he became belligerent and denied that there was anything to be concerned about. Maura's Ideal Future was for her brother to stop drinking. Her Pattern-Breaking Path centered on an intervention. She thought that if several family members confronted her brother about his problem, he might wake up to how destructive his behavior had become.

When I asked Maura to think ahead about the possible unintended consequences of her PBP on her brother, she realized that her plan was likely to backfire.

Aside from Mike's defensiveness and denial, there was another problem: many of the members of her family whom she hoped to recruit to confront her brother had their own problems with drinking. In fact, that had given rise to a different, related conflict. The one attempt she had made with her family to discuss what to do had ended in loud disagreement and more than a few hurt feelings. The attitude each family member took toward Mike's problem was heavily influenced by his or her own relationship with alcohol.

Taking that history into account, Maura realized that even if she could corral enough members of her family for an intervention, her brother would probably accuse the pot of calling the kettle black and then shut down, which would set her back from achieving her Ideal Future, rather than moving toward it.

Maura identified an unintended consequence this way:

* After we confront him about his drinking, my brother may explode and refuse to talk to me for months.

Prevent and Prepare

Once you've anticipated any possible unintended consequences of your actions, find ways to mitigate them. You can do this in two ways: you can work to *prevent* unintended consequences from happening in the first place, and you can *prepare* for how to respond if, despite your efforts, unintended consequences do occur.

For each of the unintended consequences that Bob anticipated, he thought about how he could try to prevent them from occurring at all and also how he could prepare to respond in case they did occur. Here is the plan he made:

* When I ask Sally to meet, she may agree, but in the meeting, she might get upset and start screaming at me again.

    Prevent: This time I will let Sally know in advance about the package I am presenting, to help her feel more in control and less likely to get angry in the meeting.

    Prevent: I'll send Sally an email a few days ahead of our conversation saying that I hope we'll both do our parts to ensure a thoughtful, respectful conversation.

    Prepare: If she starts screaming at me, I'll take three deep breaths and suggest that we take a break and come back when we've both cooled off.

✳ Sally may still be too angry to discuss the package with me.

Prevent: When I ask Sally to meet, I will let her know that I understand if she is still upset and that I look forward to hearing her perspective.

Prepare: If Sally says she isn't ready to discuss the package with me, I will let her know that although we do need to meet within the next two weeks because the CFO and our investors are waiting for an answer, she should let me know what days, times, and location work best for her.

✳ Even if we agree on a new compensation package now, a few months from now, Sally may be unhappy with her financial situation and decide to leave for a competing firm.

Prevent: As part of Sally's new compensation package, I will entice her to stay with additional nonmonetary benefits and give her more of the autonomy I know she craves.

Prepare: If Sally hints that she may want to leave, I'll ask to discuss it with her before she makes a final decision.

For Maura, thinking ahead about the possible unintended consequences of her actions helped her understand that her original PBP was too ambitious. She revised it until she felt confident that it would not backfire.

✳ After we confront him about his drinking, my brother may explode and refuse to talk to me for months.

Prevent: Instead of asking my family members to talk with Mike about his drinking, I will begin by slowly rebuilding my relationship with him. I'll ask him to go to a baseball game together, which we often did when we were kids. If he agrees, I'll buy us tickets.

Prevent: Before I talk with Mike about his drinking, I will discuss it with his wife, who I know is concerned about him and with whom I have a close relationship.

* If I take Mike to a baseball game, he may drink too much. I'll become worried about him, and we could get into a fight.

Prevent: Rather than asking Mike to a baseball game where alcohol consumption is usual, I'll ask him if he wants to play golf instead.

Prepare: If I sense that Mike is drunk when we're together, I will help him if needed, but I will not reprimand him.

Maura's revised PBP included plans to reach out to Mike to rebuild their relationship. She imagined having a loving, heart-to-heart conversation with him, rather than the "surprise attack" family-wide intervention of her original PBP.

Maura started by asking Mike to play weekly rounds of golf with her, which helped reestablish their previously dormant relationship. She also talked to Mike's wife and began to better understand what their home life was like. Maura's sister-in-law had some good ideas about what would and wouldn't work in terms of talking to Mike about his drinking.

One night, after a round of golf, Maura asked Mike if he'd like to join her for dinner at the golf club. He agreed, and they had a different kind of conversation than they normally did. The quiet ambiance was more conducive to a heart-to-heart conversation than their usual rowdy extended-family dinners. Maura asked Mike how things were going for him. He told her how hard things were at work and how his three young kids required his full attention, which made life difficult for him. At first, Maura just listened. Then she asked Mike how she could help him.

He revealed that he knew his drinking wasn't good for the family but he didn't think he could stop. Again Maura just listened. But a few weeks later, during another dinner together, she offered to introduce him to a friend of hers who had recently gotten sober, if he was interested. He agreed, and she introduced him to her friend. When Mike joined Alcoholics Anonymous a few months later, her family had no idea how she'd convinced him to go. Maura knew that it had taken more than a little patience, love, and foresight.

Conduct Mini-Experiments

When I was in graduate school, my colleagues and I learned that it was often best to test our hypotheses in the lab before testing them in the real world. You have more control over variables in the lab; in the real world, things can quickly get messy.

It's the same when you're testing your path. Your lab can be any place in which you'd feel safe making a mistake. The defining feature of your "lab" is the people you choose to be in it: ideally, people who care about you and who will forgive you if your experiments don't turn out the way you intend.

Your lab is for conducting small experiments in a safe environment, not grand ones.

Just as a scientist records the outcome of an experiment, you should note the results of your experiment. Did it go the way you intended? What did you learn? How will the results of your experiment influence the actions you take in the real world?

For example, if your PBP involves voicing an unpopular opinion to your boss, first practice by voicing an unpopular opinion to a friend—someone who will forgive you if your words don't come out exactly the way you intend. Notice the results of your experiment: How does your friend respond? Are your words helpful or not? How can you improve for next time?

When you conduct mini-experiments, you will gain two things: practice and immediate feedback. If you've got the luxury of having enough time to practice, you can flex your "muscles" by trying new behaviors and even develop the "muscle memory" needed to change ingrained habits. You'll also learn about the impact of your behavior—how others receive it. You can use that feedback to refine your approach in the situation where it matters most.

I once coached the CEO of a manufacturing company, Pete, who learned that his executive team was angry with him, some so much so that they were poised to quit. The message from his 360-degree feedback was overwhelming: he was a terrible listener. He issued directives, and if anyone tried to raise concerns or questions, he only issued them louder. After receiving his 360-degree feedback, Pete reluctantly admitted that he had been getting the same feedback his entire life, starting as a kid on the playground, where he would tell all the other kids what to do. "No, I don't always listen. But that's because I know I'm never going to hear anything that's going to change my mind!" he said. I pushed him, "That may be true, but tell me, what's the cost of continuing not to listen to your people?"

"I may lose key members of my executive team, people that will be hard to replace quickly. It could hurt my business," he said.

His Pattern-Breaking Path involved learning to listen, but he and I both knew that his old habits were so well established that it would take serious practice to change them.

He decided to experiment at home by listening more thought-fully to his spouse and children. At first, it was challenging not to interrupt them. But with a goal of simply listening to each of them at least once a day, he began to get better at it. He learned things about each of them that in more than a decade of marriage and fa-therhood he had never known. And for the first time, each of them felt truly listened to. Though his family benefited (and therefore willingly overlooked any awkwardness arising from the experi-ment), the other beneficiaries were Pete's direct reports, who fi-nally felt appreciated by their boss.

To experiment, find a safe laboratory for your efforts. Recall Bob, whose reactive anger exacerbated his conflict with Sally. He wanted to work on putting a pause between his experience of anger and his expression of it. He decided that he would run a series of mini-experiments to put the pause into place whenever he felt his anger get triggered by one of his engineers.

That seemed like a safe enough laboratory in which to experi-ment; Bob knew the engineers well, and he sometimes talked and joked around with them. He knew they'd stand by him no matter what and that if his experiments worked, they would appreciate the decrease in the number of angry phone calls they got from him.

At first, Bob's experimenting was hard. He forgot he was doing the experiments and he'd have a knee-jerk reaction, picking up the phone and yelling at one of the engineers. But over time, he remembered his commitment to experimenting. When he got bad news from a client, he took three deep breaths and refrained from picking up the phone to yell at the engineers. He took a walk around the block to cool off and waited until he felt centered and ready to have a calm conversation with the person responsible for that day's client mishap.

It started to work. Bob began to get positive feedback from the engineers. They seemed happier to see him and less scared of him. The outcomes of Bob's mini-experiments showed him that he was on the right track and increased his confidence that he'd eventually be able to use the pause in his interactions with Sally as well.

Now that we've looked at how to test your path, the final chapter of the book will help ensure that you reach an Optimal Outcome.

Chapter Summary

* Every action you take (or don't take) creates both intended and unintended effects. In a challenging situation, those effects become exaggerated. Your negative attributions about others can lead you to assume the worst of others, and others' attributions about you can cause even the most unintentional of your own actions to have outsized negative impacts on how other people view you.

* It is critical to think through the potential unintended impacts of your actions and inaction, so you can prevent or mitigate them. If you don't do this, no matter how carefully you've thought through your PBP, you risk making things even worse than they already are.

* Think ahead about the potential impact of your actions or inaction on yourself *and* on others, both now and in the future.

* There are two ways to mitigate potential unintended consequences: you can work to *prevent* them from happening

in the first place, and you can *prepare* for how to respond if they do occur.

✳ To create the outcome you intend, begin by testing small pattern-breaking actions in a safe environment, review your results, and adjust as needed.

Apply the Practice

TEST YOUR PATH

✳ *Think ahead.* What might be some unintended consequences of your PBP? How will you prevent and prepare for those?

✳ *Experiment.* What mini-experiments will you conduct? Who will be part of your laboratory?

✳ *Review.* Note the results of your mini-experiments. Did they go the way you intended? What did you learn? How will the results of your experiments influence the actions you take when the stakes are higher?

You can download a worksheet to help you think
ahead and conduct mini-experiments at:
optimaloutcomesbook.com/testyourpath

✻

Choose an Optimal Outcome

Dreams and reality are opposites. Action synthesizes them.

—ASSATA SHAKUR

You may be excited to pursue your Ideal Future and Pattern-Breaking Path, but if you're like many people, you may still feel hesitant. Making a change in your behavior, which your PBP will naturally require you to do, can seem daunting, even scary. When Bob was getting ready to ask Sally to meet, he almost decided not to go through with it, worried that meeting would just make things worse.

The thoughts running through his head, which may also be running through yours, were "This is so different from anything I've ever done before. This is crazy! What if it doesn't work? Should I really go through with it?"

These questions are easier to answer if you understand the sources of your hesitation. Once you do, it will be much clearer whether, and how, you should move ahead with your Pattern-Breaking Path. If you want to achieve an Optimal Outcome, it may be necessary to deal with any sources of hesitation standing in your way.

Sources of Hesitation

There are four common sources of hesitation. Though each of them is slightly different, they all serve one purpose: to keep you safely within your comfort zone. Unfortunately, staying in your comfort zone keeps you stuck in the conflict loop, which prevents you from achieving an Optimal Outcome.

Your Ideal Future Is Not Feasible, but You Fantasize About It Anyway

I met Roxanne when I was invited to consult with the senior team of a global financial services company to help figure out why the teams that reported to the four senior vice presidents were failing to collaborate. As is often the case, the toxicity started at the top: the SVPs themselves were constantly fighting and stonewalling one another's efforts. Though they said they wanted to work things out, in reality, they spoke badly behind one another's backs and didn't tell one another the truth about why they thought their teams couldn't collaborate. In addition, though they never discussed it, two of them confided to me separately that each wanted to be the one to succeed the current CEO, who was scheduled to retire within five years.

The sharpest and most sympathetic of the four SVPs was Roxanne, who had worked up the ranks for more than eighteen years at the company and was now feeling stuck. According to Roxanne, the CEO—whom she hoped to succeed—contributed to the dynamic by spending more time playing golf with Roxanne's three fellow SVPs (all men) than he did in his well-appointed office.

When I asked Roxanne to describe her Ideal Future, she told me she imagined having deep, honest relationships with her CEO and each of the other SVPs. She designed a Pattern-Breaking Path that would allow her to work with the SVPs and CEO in a spirit of true dialogue, engaging in honest conversations about the business and their relationships with one another. She knew they would need to do this in order to obtain the results their shareholders expected of them. She imagined in detail exactly how this new future would come to fruition.

However, when I asked her to tell me what would make her Pattern-Breaking Path different from past efforts, I learned that she had already invested significant time, energy, and financial resources in engaging in difficult conversations with the SVPs and the CEO, which had been facilitated by the CEO's executive coach over the span of several years, and nothing had helped. Her PBP wasn't pattern breaking at all. It was the same old, same old.

It took Roxanne several years to recognize that no matter how much she tried to get her fellow SVPs and their CEO to talk honestly with one another, it wasn't going to happen. There was too much distrust among them, the CEO was checked out and wasn't going to help, and all the failed past efforts only compounded the hopelessness each of them felt about the situation.

Like Roxanne, if you try to pursue an unfeasible Ideal Future, it may not necessarily make things worse, but you typically won't make any headway, either. You'll stay stuck in conflict by default.

As we've discussed, there is a fine line between a successful "I Have a Dream" speech about a future that inspires you and an unattainable fantasy.

There are two reasons why this line can sometimes be tough to distinguish. The first is that, like Roxanne, if you tend to be highly committed to working things out with others, you may believe that your Ideal Future is achievable, even if you've already tried in vain to achieve it multiple times.

Especially if your conflict habit is Relentlessly Collaborate, even if you thought ahead about unintended consequences in Practice 7, your Ideal Future may not be taking into account the reality of the situation you're facing. If that's the case, this chapter will help you learn how to align your Ideal Future with reality.

A second, more complicated reason is that, as Roxanne did, you may have unconsciously devised an unfeasible Ideal Future as a way to stay psychologically and emotionally safe. Imagining an Ideal Future that you know, at some level of your awareness, will never pan out allows you to feel good—you are "trying to work on things," after all—while you avoid the pain of having to make a real change. Because you unconsciously know that your Ideal Future will exist only in your imagination, it remains a safe distraction. It will never push you out of your comfort zone.

Your Walk-Away Alternative Is Unfeasible, but You Fantasize About It Anyway

Whereas the first source of hesitation is fantasizing about an unfeasible Ideal Future, the second source is fantasizing about an unfeasible Walk-Away Alternative.

A Walk-Away Alternative is any scenario you can imagine to free yourself from conflict that involves walking away from, or ending a relationship with, people in your situation.

One reason we get stuck on the conflict loop is that our Walk-Away Alternatives seem terrible to us. If they didn't, we could easily free ourselves from conflict by walking away from the other people involved and doing something else instead! But in recurring conflicts, walking away tends to have so many costs associated with it that our choices seem constrained, and the conflict becomes very difficult to escape.

This was true for Bob. He didn't think he'd ever pursue the Walk-Away Alternative of firing Sally, because if he did, he was sure he'd lose whatever friendship they had left and he'd also lose all the client relationships and institutional knowledge that would walk out the door along with her. Those were costs he was unwilling to pay. In fact, that alternative seemed so costly to him that it appeared to be unfeasible. It did not provide him with a path for freeing himself from the conflict with Sally.

The ironic thing is that an alternative's costliness or lack of feasibility doesn't seem to stop us from fantasizing about it. For instance, lack of feasibility didn't prevent Bob from fantasizing about firing Sally. When he got nervous about moving ahead with his Pattern-Breaking Path, fantasizing about firing Sally quelled his anxiety to some degree. It distracted him from his nervousness about taking new and different actions, and it also distracted him from having to deal with his feelings of anger, frustration, and sadness, all of which had intensified as a result of staying stuck in conflict.

As was true for Bob, allowing ourselves to fantasize about an unfeasible Walk-Away Alternative can leave us feeling better in the moment. It can serve as a soothing pain reliever of sorts, because it distracts us from the fear that naturally arises when we anticipate changing our behavior and pursuing our Ideal Future. Fantasizing about an unfeasible Walk-Away Alternative also distracts us from, and therefore can dampen, the painful emotions that being stuck in conflict naturally produces, including frustration, anger, disgust, guilt, and sadness.

The problem is that being distracted by our fantasies prevents us from doing any real work to improve our situation, thereby keeping us (and others) stuck in conflict.

Recall Tara, who was in conflict with her boss, Javier, and her colleague, Akiko, about who would become the company's next chief operating officer. One day, Tara told me about a Walk-Away Alternative she'd been considering: to pursue a job working for Dante, the CEO of her agency's biggest competitor.

When she revealed this to me, I asked her if she was going to follow up with Dante on the opportunity. She replied that she had already done so several times over the past few years and that each time, she and Dante had agreed, for a variety of reasons, that she wasn't the right fit for his organization.

Ironically, the fact that Tara had already explored the opportunity *and* had agreed that it wasn't the right fit for her, didn't stop her from telling me how wonderful Dante was and what a great working relationship she knew she would have with him if they ever got the chance to work together.

Fantasizing about that alternative may have distracted Tara from the pain of the current situation with Javier and Akiko, but it did nothing to help free her or anyone else from the conflict. On the contrary, it kept her stuck, fantasizing in her own mind while doing nothing to improve her situation in real life.

The insidious thing about fantasizing is that we're rarely conscious of the fact that we're doing it or of how it is keeping us stuck. Only when I invited Tara to tell me more about the possibility of a job with Dante's firm was she able to acknowledge that it wasn't a viable alternative.

It can be hard to admit that our Walk-Away Alternatives are not feasible, because when we do, we know we'll need to face up to the reality of our current situation.

Your Walk-Away Alternative Seems Unfeasible, but It's Better than Your Ideal Future

The third source of hesitation is due to assuming that a Walk-Away Alternative is unfeasible when it may actually be more feasible than pursuing your Ideal Future.

When I asked Roxanne what she would do if she left the company, she told me she sometimes thought about the possibility of finding a top job at a different company but that she didn't take this alternative seriously because she assumed that the costs of pursuing it, both to herself and to her family, would be too high.

She believed that her Walk-Away Alternative would require moving to a new city, and she didn't want to have to pay all the transaction costs she knew moving would entail: the moving process itself, transferring her kids to new schools, making new friends, and finding new doctors, all on top of having to climb the corporate ladder again in a new place.

However, when she compared the costs of her Walk-Away Alternative with those of her Ideal Future, she was startled to find that the costs she'd pay if she moved cities seemed to be *lower* than those of staying at her current company.

Though she wasn't looking forward to dealing with all the costs that moving would entail, she was able to see that the frustration of continually trying and failing to improve her current situation was far worse.

Do you have a Walk-Away Alternative that may be more feasible and less costly than you originally thought, especially compared with your Ideal Future?

Fear of Change and Comfort in Conflict

All the previous sources of hesitation notwithstanding, by far the most common reason we hesitate is that the prospect of changing our behavior to pursue an Ideal Future is intimidating or, in many cases, downright terrifying.

In our effort to avoid the discomfort that naturally accompanies changing our behavior, we neglect to realize that we'll also experience uncomfortable feelings if we *don't* move ahead.

Staying in Conflict typically produces feelings of frustration as we bang our heads against the proverbial wall, trying for the umpteenth time to improve things but failing miserably. It also perpetuates any anger, fear, sadness, or disgust arising from the conflict itself.

However, paradoxically, when conflict lasts a long time, the uncomfortable feelings that arise from it can come to seem like the "new normal." They become harder to notice, even as they deliver their full impact. Staying in Conflict can sometimes feel comfortable, even when it is, in reality, anything but.

The next section will help you take a hard look at the costs you've been paying by Staying in Conflict so you can choose whether you want to spend any more time settling for what may seem comfortable but really isn't.

The Reckoning:
Choose an Optimal Outcome

Keeping in mind the possible sources of your hesitation, compare the feasibility, and the costs and benefits, of each of your options: Ideal Future versus Staying in Conflict versus any Walk-Away Alternatives. Doing this will enable you to determine your Optimal Outcome: the best you can imagine, taking into account the reality of the other people and the situation you're facing.

Even if you don't engage in this reckoning consciously, my experience with hundreds of clients and students suggests that you'll be doing it unconsciously anyway.

But doing it *unconsciously* allows your thinking to remain unclear. Instead of making an intentional choice, you risk spending time fantasizing about your Ideal Future and your Walk-Away Alternatives while not pursuing any of them, staying stuck in conflict by default. That's a lose-lose proposition.

Becoming crystal clear about your options might mean coming face-to-face with difficult truths, but it's the only way to find an Optimal Outcome and exit the conflict loop.

Assess the Feasibility of Your Ideal Future

Ask yourself whether your Ideal Future, as you have imagined it, is viable or a pipe dream. Would anyone stand in your way, block it, or otherwise be unwilling to help you achieve it?

After years of being stuck in conflict, when Roxanne assessed the feasibility of her Ideal Future, she admitted that her hope to have honest conversations with her current SVP colleagues and CEO just didn't match the reality of the situation. They'd already tried it for years, and their efforts had failed miserably. It was time to try something different.

Assess the Costs and Benefits of Your Ideal Future

If your Ideal Future is viable, what costs do you anticipate paying if you pursue it?

Returning to Bob and Sally's situation, we can see that the biggest cost Bob anticipated paying if he pursued his Ideal Future was the discomfort he'd experience. He thought about how hard it would be for him to breathe deeply instead of yelling at Sally and the extra effort it would take to be more organized and send Sally a proposed pay package in advance of their meeting. He thought about the challenge of remembering everything he wanted to say, including starting by apologizing for his own behavior and acknowledging Sally's discomfort with the financial changes. He was concerned that if his words didn't come out right and Sally misunderstood him, he could potentially make the situation worse.

However, the potential benefits of pursuing his Ideal Future were great. They included paying Sally less as part of a new compensation package and freeing up money to reinvest in other parts of the company that were suffering; retaining Sally's expertise, company knowledge, and client relationships; and reestablishing understanding, trust, and friendship between them.

Assess the Costs and Benefits of Staying in Conflict

What costs have you already paid by Staying in Conflict? What costs are you likely to continue to pay? Are there any benefits?

Bob anticipated the pain of watching his friendship with Sally deteriorate and overpaying Sally day after day when the business needed the money elsewhere.

He had already experienced the costs involved in giving Sally the silent treatment. Not talking to her made it impossible to jointly plan and problem solve as they needed to, which led to worse outcomes for their company and clients. It was also awkward to pass her in the hallway without saying hello.

The benefits to Bob of Staying in Conflict were minimal, though he had to admit that there was something strangely comforting about it: if he didn't talk to Sally, there was no risk of upsetting her more, and he wouldn't have to try out new ways of interacting. He could be the same old Bob he had always been. Staying in Conflict brought a certain sense of comfort and relief.

Assess the Feasibility, as Well as the Costs and Benefits, of Walk-Away Alternatives

Identify any Walk-Away Alternatives you might have. Are they feasible or not?

If they're feasible, what costs might you pay if you pursued them? What might be the benefits?

Bob fantasized about firing Sally. He knew it was logistically possible, but he anticipated having to pay major costs if he did so. He feared that firing Sally would cost him their friendship, Sally's client relationships, and the institutional knowledge and expertise that she brought to her role.

The benefits of firing Sally would include paying a lower salary to her replacement and not having to deal with Sally's money issues and reactive temperament anymore.

Compare the Costs and Benefits

Once you have assessed the costs and benefits of any Walk-Away Alternatives, your Ideal Future, and Staying in Conflict, compare them with one another.

Here is an overview of Bob's comparison:

	IDEAL FUTURE: *REBUILD RELATIONSHIP AND OFFER NEW PACKAGE*	STAYING IN CONFLICT: *DO NOTHING*	WALK-AWAY ALTERNATIVE: *FIRE SALLY*
ANTICIPATED COSTS	• Need to try new behaviors • Feels scary—what if I can't do it?	• Deteriorating relationship • Still paying Sally too much • Worse outcomes for company and clients • Silence is awkward	• Long friendship gone • Client relationships gone • Company/client knowledge gone • Expertise gone
ANTICIPATED BENEFITS	• Pay less • Retain Sally's expertise and company and client knowledge • Potential for increased mutual understanding and trust	• Comfort and relief from not having to stretch myself as a leader • Won't retrigger Sally's animosity	• Hire someone for less • Don't have to deal with Sally's money issues and reactive temperament anymore

TABLE 3: Bob's Reckoning.

When you do your Reckoning, your Ideal Future *may* turn out to be your Optimal Outcome—the viable option with the lowest costs and greatest benefits—as Bob's did.

Bob saw that his hesitation was not due to a costly or unfeasible Ideal Future or PBP. His Walk-Away Alternative wasn't worth pursuing; it was way more costly than his Ideal Future. His hesitation was due to the fear that naturally arose as he anticipated the changes he would have to make to his own behavior in order to pursue his Ideal Future.

In contrast, your Walk-Away Alternative may be less costly than your Ideal Future, as Roxanne found when she wrote out her Reckoning:

	IDEAL FUTURE: *COLLABORATE*	STAYING IN CONFLICT: *DO NOTHING*	WALK-AWAY ALTERNATIVE: *FIND NEW JOB*
ANTICIPATED COSTS	• Keep getting disappointed and frustrated • Waste time and effort trying to work together with poor results • Continue to suffer financial losses when efforts to collaborate don't work • Have to deal with angry, disillusioned employees because we can't solve our differences	• Continue to suffer financial losses due to our inability to work together • Daily frustrations and anger • Have to deal with angry, disillusioned employees because we can't solve our differences	• Moving costs, including the need to find new home, doctors, friends for self and kids • Need to climb the corporate ladder again
ANTICIPATED BENEFITS	• Maybe this time will be different and we will figure out how to collaborate	• Don't need to change; can go with the flow	• Get to learn new things • Make a real impact • Experience excitement and joy again at work

TABLE 4: Roxanne's Reckoning.

Seeing this in black and white was compelling for Roxanne. She saw that her Walk-Away Alternative had lower costs and greater benefits than both her Ideal Future and Staying in Conflict. It was clear that her Walk-Away Alternative wasn't such a fantasy after all; it was her Optimal Outcome. But like Bob, she was apprehensive of change.

Identify *Your* Optimal Outcome

To identify your Optimal Outcome, assess the feasibility of your Ideal Future, Staying in Conflict, and any Walk-Away Alternatives. Compare the costs and benefits of all the feasible options with one another. The feasible option with the lowest costs and greatest benefits is your Optimal Outcome.

It is important to note that choosing to pursue an Optimal Outcome does not necessarily preclude you from exploring other options later. But if you want to free yourself from conflict, you do need to choose one option to begin with.

The following distinctions can help you identify your Optimal Outcome if you haven't done so already.

If your Ideal Future is your lowest-cost option,
call it your Optimal Outcome.
If, like Bob, your Ideal Future emerges as the lowest-cost, highest-benefit option, choose it and refer to it by its proper name: your Optimal Outcome.

If an unfeasible Walk-Away Alternative has been distracting
you from your Ideal Future, let the unfeasible fantasy go.
It is important to come face-to-face with any Walk-Away Alternatives that are simply not feasible, that don't match up with reality. This may not be easy to do, but it is necessary. Clinging to a fantasy

about an unfeasible Walk-Away Alternative is, in effect, the same as choosing to stay stuck in conflict, even if you don't consciously realize that's what you're doing.

If you've already determined that a Walk-Away Alternative is not feasible, pursuing it anyway will only cause you to become frustrated, because it will remain elusive and you'll fall back to the default, Staying in Conflict. I've seen too many good, smart people do that, and I won't let it happen to you.

As the investor Ray Dalio wrote in *Principles: Life and Work*:

> *It's essential that you embrace reality and deal with it well. Don't fall into the common trap of wishing that reality worked differently than it does or that your own realities were different. Instead, embrace your realities and deal with them effectively. . . .*
>
> *Truth—or, more precisely, an accurate understanding of reality— is the essential foundation for any good outcome.*

So face the hard truths of reality, and let go of your unfeasible Walk-Away Alternative so you can become free by taking a different, more viable path.

Though it wasn't easy, Tara acknowledged that leaving her company to work for Dante's firm was an unfeasible Walk-Away Alternative. As soon as she did so, the situation with Javier started falling into place, because for the first time, she was fully committed to making things work.

She continued to call Javier out on his bad behavior. Whenever he started screaming, Tara paused and put the spotlight back onto him, where she knew it belonged. She stopped slinking out of the room when he got into a fit, and she even asked Akiko for moral support during tough moments. Once Javier became aware of his part in their old conflict pattern and he saw that it no longer got Tara to do what he wanted, his behavior started to change, slowly but surely.

As Tara did, acknowledge what your unfeasible Walk-Away Alternative has been providing for you: a safe retreat in your mind and a salve to reduce the pain of the conflict. Remind yourself that although it may feel comfortable to stay in conflict while you daydream about an unfeasible alternative, it is only distracting you from creating a more viable Ideal Future—an Optimal Outcome—that has the potential to free you from the conflict loop for good. Let the unfeasible fantasy go.

If a Walk-Away Alternative is less costly than your Ideal Future, recognize it as your Optimal Outcome.

If, like Roxanne's, it turns out that your Walk-Away Alternative isn't so much of a fantasy after all, call it your Optimal Outcome instead. By doing so, you can free yourself from conflict in a way that may happily surprise you. Roxanne recognized that her Walk-Away Alternative was her Optimal Outcome, and she pursued it: she sought a new job with a company whose organizational culture matched her need for honest communication. She was surprised to feel a physical release in her body the moment she made the choice: her neck, which had been tight for months, suddenly felt more relaxed. She felt a lightness she hadn't felt in years. Later in the chapter, we'll see what happened for her next.

If you can find ways to lower the costs of any of your options, revise them.

Roxanne wondered whether, once she began searching in earnest, she might be able to find a new job in her current city. If that was a realistic possibility, she could lower the cost of switching jobs to practically zero.

Redesign your Pattern-Breaking Path to reflect a revised Optimal Outcome.

If you revise any of your options, you will need to update your Pattern-Breaking Path to reflect the changes. For example, because Roxanne revised her Ideal Future, she had to redesign her Pattern-Breaking Path. Instead of seeking a facilitator to mediate a conversation among her current SVP team, as her original Pattern-Breaking Path had prescribed, her revised Pattern-Breaking Path now included a phase called "Talk to headhunters" to explore job opportunities at other companies.

Be Courageous

If you have found your Optimal Outcome and you're still hesitating, remember that your discomfort is totally normal. In fact, if you didn't experience some discomfort at the thought of taking pattern-breaking action, that would be strange. We human beings naturally experience discomfort when we so much as think about breaking the patterns of the past.

It is important to remind yourself that no matter what you do—move ahead or stay put—you will experience some discomfort. The question is not whether you will experience it but which kind you will choose. Do you want to experience the discomfort that comes from engaging in new, pattern-breaking behavior? Or would you prefer to experience the discomfort of staying stuck?

The best way to deal with the discomfort is to build up your "courage muscles."

One of the most courageous turnarounds I've seen was made by a charismatic young cofounder and chief technology officer (CTO) of a SaaS company named Nico. It was a classic start-up, the brainchild of a few buddies in their twenties who had glued themselves to keyboards and built something from nothing. In just a few years, the company had grown to two hundred employees spanning three countries and had just hired its first head of talent to help prepare for Series C fundraising.

Much to Nico's surprise, the head of talent's first concern was Nico himself. To start, several employees had reported Nico for off-color humor that made them uncomfortable. (This was soon after the leadership culture of Uber was found to be riddled with sexism, which had deeply hurt Uber's market valuation and begun to draw more serious attention to gender issues in the workplace; Nico's new head of talent was rightfully sensitive to those concerns.) On top of that, Nico's colleagues felt that he often acted more like a cofounder of a small company than a CTO of a larger, growing one. He angrily seized control whenever they disagreed with him, trumping their authority and leaving them feeling dejected and effectively demoted. When the head of talent called me in to work with Nico, he shook his head. "I don't know if he's meant to be CTO at a company of this size, but see what you can do."

Nico struck me as a good guy, and I believed him when he said that he had no idea his humor had offended colleagues. "I started this company with friends who knew me well enough to know when I'm making a joke," he said. "But I guess now that we're a much larger group, I haven't thought about what that means."

The feedback about his overreach as a CTO was harder for him to take in. He was immediately defensive. "I care about this company deeply, so I get angry when I see someone doing something stupid," he said. "Also, we want people to say what they think and be transparent, and that includes me." We talked at length about how he might communicate more constructively, so that the company could make the leap from a scrappy, informal start-up to a powerful growth engine.

I'd collected 360-degree feedback and had made my own rec-ommendations to Nico. I asked him to follow up with a plan of ac-tion that we'd review together. He soon came back to me with a formal presentation that outlined the three big changes he would implement immediately, all under a general commitment to be-come a student of *sonder*, expressed in the aphorism "Be kind, for everyone you meet is fighting a great battle you know noth-ing about." His plan included learning to distinguish between his role as CTO and his role as cofounder; to build his executive pres-ence; and to give feedback to colleagues and direct reports more constructively. As he walked me through his presentation, I saw that he had made the courageous choice to stop defending himself against the feedback. He was ready to take action to improve his leadership style.

Three months later, I was sitting in the office of the head of talent, getting a fist bump. "Nice job," he said. "Nico has made a complete turnaround." When I spoke to Nico, he told me that the prospect of changing his behavior had been uncomfortable, even scary—but he had gotten through it by reminding himself that change was nec-essary if the company he had poured so much of himself into was going to succeed.

It is not only the discomfort of making change that can be diffi-cult; it is the fear of change itself. But because fear is a natural part of being human, it is not realistic to try to get rid of it. Instead, the best way to deal with fear of change is to muster your courage. As Nelson Mandela put it, "I learned that courage was not the absence of fear, but the triumph over it. The brave man is not he who does not feel afraid, but he who conquers that fear."

It may help to think about the relationship between courage and fear in scientific terms. In biology, commensalism is a type of relationship in which one organism benefits greatly from a relationship with a second one. The second organism is neither helped nor harmed by the relationship.

Courage and fear have a commensal relationship: courage needs fear in order to grow. Your courage will blossom as you overcome your fear. Your fear may diminish in the face of courage, but it will not be harmed or damaged. Fear may always be there, but courage can't grow unless fear is present. For Nico, it took fear of being ineffective and letting down the company.

You may need to talk back to your fear, as I did on the hiking trail in New Hampshire. Thank your fear for caring about you, and then tell it to leave you be.

By identifying the sources of your hesitation, talking back to your fear, and taking constructive action, you will be able to feel the discomfort and move past it.

Reap the Rewards of an Optimal Outcome

Roxanne moved her family to a new city on the West Coast. At first, as she'd expected, the transition was difficult: each member of the family, from the youngest at five to the oldest at sixteen, struggled to get used to the new environment. One of her children had trouble making new friends; another didn't find the same sports options as she'd had back east. But after a few months, Roxanne and all of her children began to find their way.

Roxanne's daily work experience made all the trouble worth the hassle: she loved her new team. They routinely engaged in honest conversations about their working relationships and about the business; it was a perfect match. And Roxanne's international experience made her stand out among her peers. She became a serious contender for succession to the CEO in anticipation of his retirement.

Tara found the courage to cede the chief marketing officer role to Akiko. She and Javier agreed to create a new role for herself: chief design officer, which would make use of her core strengths.

As for Bob, he mustered his courage and ended his silent standoff with Sally by asking if she'd be willing to meet. She agreed, and before long, they were sitting across from each other, both a bit nervous but hopeful. Bob started by saying that he wanted to discuss what had happened between them that day on the street corner and delay discussion about the compensation package itself for another day soon.

Sally nodded.

Bob took a deep breath and then told Sally that he realized he had caught her off guard on the street. He had brought up a sensitive topic without fair warning. He said that was not the kind of friend or leader he wanted to be and he was committed to doing better in the future. He told Sally that he had done a lot of reflecting over the past few months and had learned a lot.

He told her that he wanted to balance his own desire to collaborate with the need to make clear decisions as CEO of the company. He acknowledged that he was learning how to distinguish between when to collaborate and when to be more authoritative and decisive.

He then paused, looked Sally in the eye, and asked her, "Would you be willing to help me? You know, let me know when I'm doing well and when I'm bungling things?"

Sally was so surprised by Bob's question that it took her a moment to respond. A huge smile came to her face and she said, "Of course!" They discussed this for a few minutes, until Bob brought the conversation back to the issue at hand.

Bob told Sally that he recognized that she had some concerns about finances and that he wanted to understand more about them. He said he also wanted to hear if there was anything else on her mind. Then he stopped and waited for Sally to respond. There was an awkward silence while Sally mustered up the courage to speak.

She said it was clear that Bob had done a lot of thinking about the situation and that she appreciated his doing so. She acknowledged that she was concerned about her financial situation. She said that she was used to making a certain amount of money and her life was built around the assumption that it would continue. The idea that it could suddenly be yanked away from her frankly didn't seem fair.

She also said she had been upset that Bob hadn't had the decency to ask her to meet in advance, opting instead to thrust the topic on her casually as they were walking back from lunch. She added that she didn't understand why Bob had never shared the bigger picture of the company's financial situation with her. She said that when all she had heard was "Sally, we need to lower your salary!" without any rationale or background, it had been hard for her to understand why she should agree.

Now Sally waited, and another awkward silence ensued.

Bob broke the silence by telling Sally that he'd be happy to walk her through the company's financials. He said he had assumed that she wasn't interested because she had seemed so engrossed in her work selling and building client relationships. They agreed to schedule a meeting to go over the company's financials. Bob would show Sally where the business was doing well and also where it was suffering and needed financial help. He offered to send the financial overview to her in advance so she could look at it before they met. Sally seemed to appreciate his suggestion.

It then took every ounce of courage Bob had to ask Sally if she would also be willing to meet again to discuss her compensation package. He almost winced as he said it, because he was still worried that the conversation would lead to another blowup between them. But he added that this time, he'd email a proposed package to her a few days in advance so she could review it before they met.

Sally agreed, and Bob took responsibility for scheduling the two follow-up meetings, first to discuss the big-picture company financials and then to discuss the compensation package proposal.

Each of the meetings was straightforward. Though Bob's proposal represented a 10 percent decrease in Sally's bonus ceiling, it rewarded her with greater autonomy over her work. Now that she understood the bigger picture and the rationale for the decrease and also felt that she was being given the respect she deserved, she had a few questions about how and when the new package would go into effect, but agreed that it made sense.

Bob felt proud—and astonished—that the process had more or less come to fruition the way he'd imagined it. He knew there was still a long road ahead to rebuild trust and friendship with Sally, but he recognized it as a natural part of any Pattern-Breaking Path. He understood that staying free from conflict would require him to continue to be as thoughtful and courageous as he had been during the past few weeks. But unlike in the past, when he'd questioned whether or not he could do it successfully, now he knew he was up to the task.

Partly as a result of Bob's courageous efforts, a few months later, to his and his team's delight, after entertaining multiple bids, they successfully sold their company to one of the largest, most prestigious companies in their field.

An Optimal Outcome Is Contagious

When you do the practices in this book, you will free yourself from conflict.

Rather than getting mad *again* at the dirty dishes your spouse left in the sink, you'll find yourself taking a deep breath and choosing to respond differently than you have in the past.

Instead of hiding every time other people get angry at you, you'll start asking what's gotten *them* so upset.

Rather than offering people option after option even when they've rejected them all, you'll notice the signs more quickly, save everyone time and energy, and know when it's time to call it quits.

And instead of taking the blame and stewing in shame whenever someone criticizes you, you'll bounce back more quickly, recognizing that it's probably not all your fault.

Doing this will take a generous dose of courage. You'll need the wherewithal to try things out, possibly fail, dust yourself off, and try again. You'll learn that a Pattern-Breaking Path isn't always a straight road, but it is a rewarding one.

Taking a Pattern-Breaking Path will free you from the conflict loop. But the magical part is that once you're free, and the conflict pattern has been broken, others will naturally become free from it as well. As Nelson Mandela said, "For to be free is not merely to cast off one's chains, but to live in a way that respects and enhances the freedom of others."

Your actions are a contagious form of leadership; when you free yourself from conflict, you help free others as well.

Chapter Summary

* There are four common sources of hesitation. Though each of them is slightly different, they all serve one purpose: to keep you safely within your comfort zone. Unfortunately, staying in your comfort zone keeps you stuck in the con-

flict loop, which prevents you from achieving an Optimal Outcome.

* The first source of hesitation is due to fantasizing about an unfeasible Ideal Future. If your Ideal Future does not take into account the reality of your situation or the needs of other people, it won't work, and you'll stay stuck in conflict by default.

* The second source of hesitation is due to fantasizing about a Walk-Away Alternative regardless of how costly or unfeasible it is. A Walk-Away Alternative is any scenario that would involve walking away from, or ending a relationship with, people in your situation.

* Fantasizing about a Walk-Away Alternative can serve as a pain reliever, distracting you from the fear of changing your behavior and the painful emotions of being stuck in conflict. But being distracted by your fantasies keeps you from doing any real work to improve your situation, thereby keeping you and others stuck in conflict.

* The third source of hesitation occurs when your Walk-Away Alternative is more feasible than you originally thought, especially compared with your Ideal Future. You may spin your wheels trying to make your Ideal Future work while ignoring the fact that walking away is actually a more viable choice.

* The fourth and by far most common source of hesitation is that the prospect of changing your behavior to pursue

your Pattern-Breaking Path is daunting. In your effort to avoid this discomfort, you neglect to take into account the fact that you'll also experience uncomfortable feelings if you *don't* move ahead.

* When conflict lasts a long time, the uncomfortable feelings that arise from it can come to seem like the "new normal." They become harder to notice. Staying in Conflict can sometimes feel comfortable, even when it is, in reality, anything but.

* To identify an Optimal Outcome, assess the feasibility of your Ideal Future, Staying in Conflict, and any Walk-Away Alternatives and compare each of the feasible options' costs and benefits with one another. The feasible option with the lowest costs and greatest benefits is your Optimal Outcome.

* It is not realistic to try to get rid of your fear of change. Experiencing fear of change is a natural part of being human. Instead, the best way to deal with fear of change is to muster up your courage. Your courage will blossom as you overcome your fear.

* Taking a Pattern-Breaking Path to achieve an Optimal Outcome will free you from the conflict loop. Once you're free, the conflict pattern will be broken, and others will naturally be freed from it as well.

* Your actions are a contagious form of leadership; when you free yourself from conflict, you help free others, too.

Apply the Practice

CHOOSE AN OPTIMAL OUTCOME

❋ *Identify any hesitation.* What sources of hesitation are at play for you, if any?

❋ *Reckon with the options.* What are the feasibility, costs, and benefits of your Ideal Future, Staying in Conflict, and any Walk-Away Alternatives?

❋ *Identify your Optimal Outcome.* Which of the feasible options (Ideal Future, Staying in Conflict, and any Walk-Away Alternatives) has the greatest benefits and lowest costs for you? This is your Optimal Outcome. Design a Pattern-Breaking Path to pursue it.

❋ *Be courageous.* What is one courageous action you can take to follow your Pattern-Breaking Path toward an Optimal Outcome?

❋ *Learn.* If this helps you exit the conflict loop, congratulations. If it doesn't, pause and design and test another path until you free yourself from the loop.

You can download a Reckoning Template at:
optimaloutcomesbook.com/reckoning

How to Achieve an Optimal Outcome

PART I	UNDERSTANDING THE CONFLICT LOOP
Practice 1	Notice Your Conflict Habits and Patterns
PART II	BREAKING THE CONFLICT PATTERN
Practice 2	Increase Clarity and Complexity: Map Out the Conflict
Practice 3	Put Your Emotions to Work for You
Practice 4	Honor Ideal and Shadow Values— Yours and Theirs
PART III	FREEING YOURSELF FROM THE LOOP
Practice 5	Imagine Your Ideal Future
Practice 6	Design a Pattern-Breaking Path (PBP)
Practice 7	Test Your Path
Practice 8	Choose an Optimal Outcome

Appendix 1: Values Inventory

This Values Inventory is adapted from Stewart D. Friedman's *Total Leadership: Be a Better Leader, Have a Richer Life* and Robert J. Lee and Sara N. King's *Discovering the Leader in You: A Guide to Realizing Your Personal Leadership Potential.* I have edited and added to it over the years, based on student and client feedback, to help it speak to as diverse an audience as possible. It is by no means exhaustive; please add your own values as you see fit. Interested readers can find a printable version of this Values Inventory at optimaloutcomesbook.com/valuesinventory

Values Inventory

Achievement: a sense of accomplishment or mastery

Advancement: growth, seniority, and promotion resulting from work well done

Adventure: new and challenging opportunities, excitement, risk

Aesthetics: appreciation of beauty in things, ideas, and surroundings

Affiliation: interaction with other people, recognition as a member of a group, belonging

Affluence: high income, financial success, prosperity

Authority: position and power to control events and other people's activities

Autonomy: ability to act independently with few constraints; self-reliance

Challenge: continually facing complex and demanding tasks and problems

Change and variation: absence of routine; unpredictability

Collaboration: close, cooperative working relationships with groups

Community: serving and supporting a purpose that supersedes personal desires

Competency: demonstrating high proficiency and knowledge

Competition: rivalry with winning as the goal

Courage: taking action in the face of fear

Creativity: discovering, developing, or designing new ideas or things; demonstrating imagination

Curiosity: a desire to learn or know things

Diverse perspectives: ideas and opinions that open up new pathways and illuminate new opportunities

Duty: respect for authority, rules, and regulations

Economic security: steady and secure employment, adequate reward, low risk, ability to afford basic needs

Enjoyment: fun, joy, and laughter

Family: spending time with partner, children, parents, extended family

Friendship: close personal relationships with others

Health: physical and mental well-being, vitality

Helping others: helping people attain their goals; providing care and support

Humor: the ability to laugh at yourself and at life

Influence: having an impact on the attitudes or opinions of others

Inner harmony: happiness, contentment, being at peace with yourself

Justice: fairness, doing the right thing

Knowledge: the pursuit of understanding, skill, and expertise; continual learning

Location: choice of a place to live that is conducive to a desired lifestyle

Love: involvement in close, affectionate relationships; intimacy

Loyalty: faithfulness; dedication to individuals, traditions, or organizations

Order: stability, routine, predictability, clear lines of authority, standardization

Personal development: dedication to maximizing potential

Physical fitness: maintaining health through physical activity and nutrition

Recognition: positive feedback and public credit for work well done; respect and admiration

Responsibility: dependability, accountability for results

Safety: physical, mental, or emotional freedom from harm or danger

Self-respect: pride, self-esteem, sense of knowing oneself

Spirituality: strong spiritual or religious beliefs, moral fulfillment

Status: being respected for a job or an association with a prestigious group or organization

Trustworthiness: being known as reliable and sincere

Wisdom: sound judgment based on knowledge, experience, and understanding

Appendix 2:
How to Apply the Practices
to Teams and Organizations

I've spent the past twenty years consulting with leaders and teams in organizations, including Fortune 500 companies, growing start-ups, universities, international nonprofits, and governmental agencies, helping them achieve Optimal Outcomes. As an organizational psychologist, I know that it is possible, and necessary, to work at multiple levels simultaneously—with individuals, their teams, and the whole organization—to help people break free from existing conflict patterns and achieve individual, team, and organizational Optimal Outcomes. I've written a short bonus chapter showing how to use the practices to create Optimal Outcomes for your team and organization.

You can download this chapter at optimaloutcomesbook.com /teams

Acknowledgments

T his book would not exist without the loving guidance and
support of many people. There are no words to express my
gratitude to my parents, Joan and Hank Goldman, who
taught me that I could achieve anything I set my mind to. And to
my late grandparents, Helen and Hans Goldman and Florence
and Benjamin Schachat, whose love and hard work helped make
my dreams a reality. For showing me that being an organizational
psychologist is the best job in the world, I honor my late uncle Dr.
Robert Schachat.

I am grateful for all I learned at the start of my career at the Program on Negotiation at Harvard Law School. In particular, I feel
indebted for the world-class training and advice I received from
Roger Fisher, Bruce Patton, Doug Stone, Sheila Heen, Dan Shapiro,
John Richardson, Erica Ariel Fox, and Bob Bordone.

My thanks to the father of conflict resolution, Dr. Morton
Deutsch, who was not only a brilliant researcher and theorist but

also a caring teacher, mentor, and friend, and to my graduate adviser, Dr. Peter T. Coleman, who continues to provide the foundations that have allowed me, and my work, to thrive. This book could never have been written without both Mort's and Peter's example, support, dedication, and stewardship.

My thanks to the entire faculty and staff at the Program in Social-Organizational Psychology at Teachers College, Columbia University, for being such a wonderful home for so many years.

Thanks to Dr. Joel Brockner for providing another place to call home across the street at Columbia Business School Executive Education and for sharing stories about the mentor I never got the chance to know, Dr. Jeffrey Z. Rubin. To Dr. Sinaia Nathanson, who taught the course at Tufts that launched my career in 1996, and to Dr. Anthony Wanis-St. John for suggesting that I might want to study with Mort.

Thanks to the founding members of the Social and Behavioral Sciences Division at the US Department of Homeland Security, especially Dr. Joshua Sinai and Dr. Allison G. Smith, and to Dr. Arie Kruglanski, Dr. Gary Ackerman, and Dr. Kate Izsak at the National Center for the Study of Terrorism and Responses to Terrorism (NC-START) at the University of Maryland, for providing the original research funding and support that has culminated in this book.

Thanks to Dr. Evelin Lindner, the founder of Human Dignity and Humiliation Studies, whose research on emotions and conflict was the inspiration for my own.

Thank you to the faculty and staff at the Morton Deutsch International Center for Cooperation and Conflict Resolution at Columbia. My thanks to Dr. Peter T. Coleman and Dr. Beth Fisher-Yoshida for originally giving me the opportunity to teach Optimal Outcomes; Dr. Claudia Cohen and Danielle Coon for helping me expand the course; Molly Clark and Kim Nguyen for supporting the course and the students; my long-standing teaching assistant and coach, Rebecca Toffolon James; and our amazing coaching team, including Kailen Krame, Pervis Taylor III, Scott Hannon, Annie-Lou St-Amant, Michelle McGowan, Lauren Schadt, Ana Perea, John Sanchez, and Esther Azar.

To the hundreds of Columbia University students from all over the world and from diverse professional disciplines who, over ten years, shared their stories, vulnerabilities, and inner wisdom and who, by their example, showed me what it really means to become free from conflict. Special thanks to Robert Louis-Charles, Cheryl Bucci, Yajini Baluja, Bill Bokoff, and Leigh Winters.

Thank you to Jeffrey Walker for introducing me to Dinabandhu Sarley and to Dinabandhu and 1440 Multiversity for the opportunity to teach the Optimal Outcomes workshop with nonprofit executives. Thanks to Eden Abrahams, Jo Ilfeld, and Jon Shuster for their insight and excellent coaching, as well as to the participants who brought their whole selves to the experience.

Thank you to my colleagues, partners, and clients at Alignment Strategies Group who helped me test the Optimal Outcomes practices, especially Dr. Dana Bilsky Asher, Dr. Wendy K. Smith, Ana Perea, Allan Weiser, and all those who will remain anonymous.

Thanks to Sarah Hinawi, Susan Leon, Patty Chang Anker, and Ken Anker for early advice and inspiration. Gratitude to my agent, Lisa DiMona, for unwavering support throughout every part of the process and for introducing me to my editor, Stephanie Hitchcock, and my publisher, Hollis Heimbouch. Lisa, Stephanie, and Hollis together expertly guided me through the publishing experience and helped make it an enjoyable adventure! Thanks to the entire HarperBusiness team, including the extraordinary Leslie Cohen, Penny Makras, and Hannah Long.

Thank you to Sara Grace and Emily Loose for their expert editing, and to graphic facilitator Tamra Carhart for her beautiful illustrations in the introduction and chapter on mapping.

Gratitude to friends and family who took the time out of their own busy work and family schedules to offer me helpful feedback on drafts of the manuscript, in some cases multiple times: Doug Stone and Sheila Heen, Adam Burgoon, Steve Fuzesi, Wendy Smith, Esther Kinderlerer, Ana Levy-Lyons, Dana Bilsky Asher, Nancy Beer, Roy Edelstein, Sarah Birkeland, Erik Hajer, Eden Abrahams, Joshua Sinai, Kailen Krame, and Emily Spuza. And to my husband, Jeff Wetzler, and my parents, Joan and Hank Goldman, for their helpful feedback throughout.

For their advice and support over many years, deep gratitude to Diana Smith and Bruce Patton, Amy Elizabeth Fox and all those at Mobius Executive Leadership, Gal Yaguri, Susan Dominus, Rabbis Shoshana Leis and Ben Newman, Max and Eve Koltuv, Rachael O'Meara, and Melanie Hoopes.

For their generous collaboration on the University of Chicago's Defining Wisdom Grant, which formed the original seed of this work, thanks to Aliki Nicolaides, Riva Kantowitz, and Susan Allen Nan.

For their long-standing support and love, thanks to Pat and John Wetzler, David and Suzanne Goldman, Arielle and Jon Richter, Lauren Wetzler and Steve Fuzesi, Rafe Jenney, Anne Hamburger, Maureen DePass, Alex Lopez, the Boston Chevra, and the Riverdale Girls.

Thanks to everyone who listened to, laughed about, cried at, and gave feedback on the TEDx talk, including Kimberly Marcus, Lisa DiMona, Cassandra Sweet, Adam Burgoon, Heidi Frieze, Frank Faranda, Sarah Jackson, Lara Weitzman, Sarah Rosengaertner, Risa Kaufman, Amy Stern, Patty Goldstick, Gal Yaguri, Dana

Bilsky Asher, Jennifer Mittleman, Beth Pocius, and the organizers and speakers at TEDxChelseaPark.

To Romemu, Lab/Shul, and Shtiebel for creating the sanctuaries that gave these ideas roots and wings, sometimes in the quietest of moments.

To my coaches over the years who helped bring this project to fruition: Marcie Mac Kinnon Gorfinkle, Erik Hajer, Jim Fyfe, Sue Campbell, Kelsey Crouch, and Cesar Bravo.

Thanks to Emily Spuza for her heroic support and friendship over many years.

Thank you to my friend and mentor Erica Ariel Fox for shining the light on this journey from the beginning.

To my husband, Jeff, thank you for your love and for being a rock for our family and me and for so many others. I could not have done this without you. And to our children, Jacob and Eden, for being exactly who you are. Thank you to Eden for designing the model first cover for the book and to Jacob for rescuing my computer and printer again and again. And to you both for asking with genuine care at such young ages, "How's the book going, Mom?" and for cheering and celebrating with me at every stage.

And finally, gratitude to the divine presence in all of us and to you, the reader, for being part of this journey. May all your paths be blessed, and may your outcomes be optimal.

Notes

＊

INTRODUCTION

7   two men: Roger Fisher, Bruce Patton, and William Ury, *Getting to Yes: Negotiating Agreement Without Giving In* (New York: Penguin Books, 2011).

7   *Difficult Conversations*: Douglas Stone, Bruce Patton, and Sheila Heen, *Difficult Conversations: How to Discuss What Matters Most* (New York: Portfolio Penguin, 2011).

8   And I discovered research: Evelin Gerda Lindner, "Healing the Cycles of Humiliation: How to Attend to the Emotional Aspects of 'Unsolvable' Conflicts and the Use of 'Humiliation Entrepreneurship,'" *Peace and Conflict: Journal of Peace Psychology* 8, no. 2 (June 2002): 125–38.

9   more creative, innovative: Sylvia Ann Hewlett, Melinda Marshall, and Laura Sherbin, "How Diversity Can Drive Innovation," *Harvard Business Review*, December 2013, https://hbr.org/2013/12/how-diversity-can-drive-innovation

9   and productive: Vivian Hunt, Dennis Layton, and Sara Prince, "Diversity Matters," McKinsey & Company, February 2, 2015, https://www.mckinsey.com/business-functions/organization/our-insights/why-diversity-matters

10 Campbell says that: Joseph Campbell, *The Hero with a Thousand Faces*, 3rd ed. (Novato, CA: New World Library, 2008).

10   it's self-perpetuating: Morton Deutsch, *The Resolution of Conflict: Constructive and Destructive Processes* (New Haven, CT: Yale University Press, 1973).

12   Today, mindfulness: Jon Kabat-Zinn, *Wherever You Go, There You Are: Mindfulness Meditation in Everyday Life* (New York: Hachette Books, 2014).

12   *Pausing* is a mindfulness practice: Rachael O'Meara, *Pause: Harnessing the Life-Changing Power of Giving Yourself a Break* (New York: TarcherPerigee, 2017).

PRACTICE 1: NOTICE YOUR CONFLICT HABITS AND PATTERNS

25   Based on research: Jennifer Goldman, *Emotions in Long-Term Conflict: The Differential Effects of Collective-Versus Personal-Level Humiliating Experiences* (n.p.: LAP Lambert Academic Publishing, 2014).

25   As Doug Stone: Douglas Stone, Bruce Patton, and Sheila Heen, *Difficult Conversations: How to Discuss What Matters Most* (New York: Portfolio Penguin, 2011).

25   performance improves: Giada Di Stefano, Francesca Gino, Gary P. Pisano, and Bradley R. Staats, "Making Experience Count: The Role of Reflection in Individual Learning," Harvard Business School Working Paper 14–093, June 14, 2016, https://www.hbs.edu/faculty /Publication%20Files/14-093_defe8327-eeb6-40c3-aafe-2619418 1cfd2.pdf

36   For example, scientific research: Bas Verplanken and Wendy Wood, "Interventions to Break and Create Consumer Habits," *Journal of Public Policy & Marketing* 25, no. 1 (Spring 2006): 90–103, https:// pdfs.semanticscholar.org/6371/64b5f2d792d8c13d6f8309c89bea00 2226e0.pdf

     David T. Neal, Wendy Wood, and Jeffrey M. Quinn, "Habits—A Repeat Performance," *Current Directions in Psychological Science* 15, no. 4 (2006): 198–202, https://dornsife.usc.edu/assets/sites/545/docs /Wendy_Wood_Research_Articles/Habits/Neal.Wood.Quinn.2006 _Habits_a_repeat_performance.pdf

36   as popularized by: Charles Duhigg, *The Power of Habit: Why We Do What We Do in Life and Business* (New York: Random House Trade Paperbacks, 2014).

36   However, as the research shows: Ibid.

38   "People who confuse": Ray Dalio, *Principles: Life and Work* (New York: Simon & Schuster, 2017).

40 Notice Your Conflict Habits and Patterns: To take an online assessment to identify your primary conflict habit and your conflict pattern with others, visit optimaloutcomesbook.com/assessment

PRACTICE 2: INCREASE CLARITY AND COMPLEXITY:
MAP OUT THE CONFLICT

49 One of the best ways: Peter Coleman, *The Five Percent: Finding Solutions to Seemingly Impossible Conflicts* (New York: Public Affairs, 2011).
49 This chapter's practice draws: Ibid.
59 Increase Clarity and Complexity: For an online template you can use to create your own conflict map, visit optimaloutcomesbook.com/map

PRACTICE 3: PUT YOUR EMOTIONS TO WORK FOR YOU

61 The creators of the film: Dacher Keltner and Paul Ekman, "The Science of 'Inside Out,'" *New York Times*, July 3, 2015, https://www.ny times.com/2015/07/05/opinion/sunday/the-science-of-inside-out .html
61 In his groundbreaking work: Paul Ekman and Wallace V. Friesen, "Constants Across Cultures in the Face and Emotion," *Journal of Personality and Social Psychology* 17, no. 2 (1971): 124–29, http://www .communicationcache.com/uploads/1/0/8/8/10887248/constants _across_cultures_in_the_face_and_emotion.pdf
62 A recent meta-survey: Paul Ekman, "What Scientists Who Study Emotion Agree About," *Perspectives on Psychological Science* 11, no. 1 (2016): 31–34, https://www.paulekman.com/wp-content/uploads /2013/07/What-Scientists-Who-Study-Emotion-Agree-About.pdf
62 Within those five: To learn more about the five emotions and the states they contain, interested readers can visit Dr. Paul Ekman's Atlas of Emotions, which is also supported by the Dalai Lama. It is the best representation of emotions I've seen; see http://atlasof emotions.org
62 the importance of emotional intelligence: Daniel Goleman, *Emotional Intelligence: A Practical Guide to Making Friends with Your Emotions and Raising Your EQ* (New York: Bantam Books, 2006).
73 The well-known Vietnamese Buddhist monk: Thich Nhat Hanh, *Being Peace* (Berkeley, CA: Parallax Press, 1996).
75 In the film *Inside Out*: To learn more about the personalities of the emotions in the film *Inside Out*, see Joseph C. Lin, "Meet the Emotions

of Pixar's *Inside Out*," *Time*, June 19, 2015, http://time.com/3924847
/pixar-disney-inside-out-emotions/

85 Put Your Emotions to Work for You: To take an online assessment to
identify the emotions trap to which you are most vulnerable, visit
optimaloutcomesbook.com/assessment

PRACTICE 4: HONOR IDEAL AND SHADOW VALUES—YOURS AND THEIRS

91 I've found it to be a powerful tool: You can also use the online version
of the Values Inventory at optimaloutcomesbook.com/valuesinventory

98 As millennials have risen: The Center for Generational Kinetics
says, "Millennials have become the largest generation in the U.S.
workforce." To learn more about intergenerational differences, visit
https://genhq.com/faq-info-about-generations/

99 Pioneering psychological research: C. M. Steele, "The Psychology
of Self-Affirmation: Sustaining the Integrity of the Self," in *Advances
in Experimental Social Psychology*, vol. 21, ed. L. Berkowitz (San Diego,
CA: Academic Press, 1988), 261–302.

106 Using the lists: If you'd like to include values for multiple people or
groups, you can find Values Map templates accommodating various
configurations of people at optimaloutcomesbook.com/valuesmaps

110 I noticed that it had: This refers to the popular Amazon Prime television show *The Marvelous Mrs. Maisel.*

111 For any gaps: For a template to help close the gap between your ideal
values and your behavior, visit optimaloutcomesbook.com/gap

113 In New York City: Technically, the scaffolding helps the workers
repair the structure and the shed protects pedestrians from debris;
see Keith Loria, "Keeping the Sky from Falling: Construction Sheds,
Exterior Scaffolds and Pedestrian Safety," The Cooperator New York,
March 2014, https://cooperator.com/article/keeping-the-sky-from
-falling/full. In a conflict situation, your metaphorical conversation
scaffolding helps you to repair your relationship and emerge unscathed.

116 Honor Ideal and Shadow Values: To download a Values Practice Packet
that will walk you through the work of this chapter, visit optimalout
comesbook.com/values

PRACTICE 5: IMAGINE YOUR IDEAL FUTURE

125 "We think, each": Daniel Kahneman, *Thinking, Fast and Slow* (New
York: Farrar, Straus and Giroux, 2011).

126 "We more intentionally value": John Paul Lederach, *The Moral Imagination: The Art and Soul of Building Peace* (Oxford, UK: Oxford University Press, 2005), 108.

127 "I Have a Dream" speech: Watch Dr. King's "I Have a Dream" speech to see how he used the five senses and emotions to help us imagine his Ideal Future. It also serves as a reminder of how far we've come and how far we still have to go to reach the Ideal Future he describes. For the full video and transcript, see Jessica Kwong, "Martin Luther King Jr.'s 'I Have a Dream' Speech: Full Text and Video," *Newsweek*, April 4, 2018, https://www.newsweek.com/mlk-jr-assassination -anniversary-i-have-dream-speech-full-text-video-870680

135 What is *your* version: For examples, visit optimaloutcomesbook.com /imagine

PRACTICE 6: DESIGN A PATTERN-BREAKING PATH (PBP)

138 Former president Barack Obama: Helene Cooper and Abby Goodnough, "Over Beers, No Apologies, but Plans to Have Lunch," *New York Times*, July 30, 2009, https://www.nytimes.com/2009/07/31/us /politics/31obama.html

140 he invited Dr. Gates and Sergeant Crowley: Astute readers will recall that then vice president Joe Biden was eventually invited to join the men as well. For more information about the Beer Summit, see ibid.

150 Design a Pattern-Breaking Path (PBP): Interested readers can download a template to help design a PBP at optimaloutcomesbook.com/PBP

PRACTICE 7: TEST YOUR PATH

153 One of history's most renowned feats: This story is narrated by Rosalynn Carter with original video footage from Camp David in the excellent documentary film about Jimmy Carter's life, *Man from Plains*.

155 In her book *10-10-10*: Suzy Welch, *10—10-10: 10 Minutes, 10 Months, 10 Years: A Life-Transforming Idea* (New York: Scribner, 2009).

166 Test Your Path: Interested readers can download a Test Your Path template at optimaloutcomesbook.com/testyourpath

PRACTICE 8: CHOOSE AN OPTIMAL OUTCOME

177 Once you have assessed: To download a blank Reckoning template, visit optimaloutcomesbook.com/reckoning

181 "it's essential that you": Ray Dalio, *Principles: Life and Work* (New York: Simon & Schuster, 2017).

190 "For to be free": Nelson Mandela, *Long Walk to Freedom* (Boston: Little, Brown and Company, 1995).

193 Choose an Optimal Outcome: To download a Reckoning template, visit optimaloutcomesbook.com/reckoning

Index

✳

About the Author

✳

JENNIFER GOLDMAN-WETZLER, PHD, is the founding principal of Alignment Strategies Group, a New York–based consulting firm, where she advises CEOs and their executive teams on how to optimize organizational health and growth. For the past two decades, Jennifer has advised senior leaders at start-ups, global corporations, and large nonprofit and governmental institutions, including Google, IBM, Oscar Health Insurance, Roche, the New School, the New York City Economic Development Corporation, and the United Nations. She also teaches conflict freedom at the Morton Deutsch International Center for Cooperation and Conflict Resolution at Columbia University. She lives outside New York City with her family.